RED CLOUD

NORTH AMERICAN INDIANS OF ACHIEVEMENT

RED CLOUD
Sioux War Chief

▼ ▼ ▼

Jerry Lazar

Senior Consulting Editor
W. David Baird
Howard A. White Professor of History
Pepperdine University

CHELSEA HOUSE PUBLISHERS

New York   Philadelphia

FRONTISPIECE Known in the Lakota tongue as Makhpya-luta, Red Cloud led
the Oglala Sioux in war and peace for more than 40 years. This photograph was
taken in 1880, when he served as head chief of Pine Ridge Agency.

ON THE COVER Wearing a medal issued by the U.S. government, Red Cloud
holds a peace pipe in this rendition of an 1880 photograph.

Chelsea House Publishers
EDITORIAL DIRECTOR Richard Rennert
EXECUTIVE MANAGING EDITOR Karyn Gullen Browne
COPY CHIEF Robin James
PICTURE EDITOR Adrian G. Allen
ART DIRECTOR Robert Mitchell
MANUFACTURING DIRECTOR Gerald Levine
ASSISTANT ART DIRECTOR Joan Ferrigno

North American Indians of Achievement
SENIOR EDITOR Marian W. Taylor
NATIVE AMERICAN SPECIALIST Jack Miller

Staff for RED CLOUD
ASSISTANT EDITOR Margaret Dornfeld
EDITORIAL ASSISTANT Sydra Mallery
PICTURE RESEARCHER Sandy Jones
COVER ILLUSTRATOR Michael Hobbs

Printed and bound in Mexico.

First Printing

1 3 5 7 9 8 6 4 2

Library of Congress Cataloging-in-Publication Data

Lazar, Jerry.
Red Cloud/Jerry Lazar.
     p. cm.—(North American Indians of achievement)
   Includes bibliographical references and index.
ISBN 0-7910-1718-4
ISBN 0-7910-2044-4 (pbk.)
1. Red Cloud, 1822–1909—Juvenile literature. 2. Oglala Indians—Biography—Juvenile lit-
erature. 3. Red Cloud's War, 1866–1867—Juvenile literature. 4. Indians of North Amer-
ica—Great Plains—Wars—Juvenile literature. [1. Red Cloud, 1822–1909. 2. Oglala
Indians—Biography. 3. Indians of North America—Biography.] I. Title. II. Series.
E99.O3R375 1995   94-22728
973'.04975'092—dc20   CIP
[B]   AC

CONTENTS

NORTH AMERICAN INDIANS OF ACHIEVEMENT

Other titles in preparation

ON INDIAN LEADERSHIP

by W. David Baird
Howard A. White Professor of History
Pepperdine University

Authoritative utterance is in thy mouth, perception is in thy heart, and thy tongue is the shrine of justice," the ancient Egyptians said of their king. From him, the Egyptians expected authority, discretion, and just behavior. Homer's *Iliad* suggests that the Greeks demanded somewhat different qualities from their leaders: justice and judgment, wisdom and counsel, shrewdness and cunning, valor and action. It is not surprising that different people living at different times should seek different qualities from the individuals they looked to for guidance. By and large, a people's requirements for leadership are determined by two factors: their culture and the unique circumstances of the time and place in which they live.

Before the late 15th century, when non-Indians first journeyed to what is now North America, most Indian tribes were not ruled by a single person. Instead, there were village chiefs, clan headmen, peace chiefs, war chiefs, and a host of other types of leaders, each with his or her own specific duties. These influential people not only decided political matters but also helped shape their tribe's social, cultural, and religious life. Usually, Indian leaders held their positions because they had won the respect of their peers. Indeed, if a leader's followers at any time decided that he or she was out of step with the will of the people, they felt free to look to someone else for advice and direction.

Thus, the greatest achievers in traditional Indian communities were men and women of extraordinary talent. They were not only skilled at navigating the deadly waters of tribal politics and cultural customs but also able to, directly or indirectly, make a positive and significant difference in the daily life of their followers.

From the beginning of their interaction with Native Americans, non-Indians failed to understand these features of Indian leadership. Early European explorers and settlers merely assumed that Indians had the same relationship with their leaders as non-Indians had with their kings and queens. European monarchs generally inherited their positions and ruled large nations however they chose, often with little regard for the desires or needs of their subjects. As a result, the settlers of Jamestown saw Pocahontas as a "princess" and Pilgrims dubbed Wampanoag leader Metacom "King Philip," envisioning them in roles very different from those in which their own people placed them.

As more and more non-Indians flocked to North America, the nature of Indian leadership gradually began to change. Influential Indians no longer had to take on the often considerable burden of pleasing only their own people; they also had to develop a strategy of dealing with the non-Indian newcomers. In a rapidly changing world, new types of Indian role models with new ideas and talents continually emerged. Some were warriors; others were peacemakers. Some held political positions within their tribes; others were writers, artists, religious prophets, or athletes. Although the demands of Indian leadership altered from generation to generation, several factors that determined which Indian people became prominent in the centuries after first contact remained the same.

Certain personal characteristics distinguished these Indians of achievement. They were intelligent, imaginative, practical, daring, shrewd, uncompromising, ruthless, and logical. They were constant in friendships, unrelenting in hatreds, affectionate with their relatives, and respectful to their God or gods. Of course, no single Native American leader embodied all these qualities, nor these qualities only. But it was these characteristics that allowed them to succeed.

The special skills and talents that certain Indians possessed also brought them to positions of importance. The life of Hiawatha, the legendary founder of the powerful Iroquois Confederacy, displays the value that oratorical ability had for many Indians in power.

The biography of Cochise, the 19th-century Apache chief, illustrates that leadership often required keen diplomatic skills not only in transactions among tribespeople but also in hardheaded negotiations with non-Indians. For others, such as Mohawk Joseph Brant and Navajo Peter MacDonald, a non-Indian education proved advantageous in their dealings with other peoples.

Sudden changes in circumstance were another crucial factor in determining who became influential in Indian communities. King Philip in the 1670s and Geronimo in the 1880s both came to power when their people were searching for someone to lead them into battle against white frontiersmen who had forced upon them a long series of indignities. Seeing the rising discontent of Indians of many tribes in the 1810s, Tecumseh and his brother, the Shawnee prophet Tenskwatawa, proclaimed a message of cultural revitalization that appealed to thousands. Other Indian achievers recognized cooperation with non-Indians as the most advantageous path during their lifetime. Sarah Winnemucca in the late 19th century bridged the gap of understanding between her people and their non-Indian neighbors through the publication of her autobiography *Life Among the Piutes*. Olympian Jim Thorpe in the early 20th century championed the assimilationist policies of the U.S. government and, with his own successes, demonstrated the accomplishments Indians could make in the non-Indian world. And Wilma Mankiller, principal chief of the Cherokees, continues to fight successfully for the rights of her people through the courts and through negotiation with federal officials.

Leadership among Native Americans, just as among all other peoples, can be understood only in the context of culture and history. But the centuries that Indians have had to cope with invasions of foreigners in their homelands have brought unique hardships and obstacles to the Native American individuals who most influenced and inspired others. Despite these challenges, there has never been a lack of Indian men and women equal to these tasks. With such strong leaders, it is no wonder that Native Americans remain such a vital part of this nation's cultural landscape.

1

MASSACRE

From the spring of 1866 to the fall of 1868, the Oglala war chief Red Cloud led a fierce campaign to drive miners, settlers, and U.S. troops from his people's hunting grounds near the Powder River. This photograph was taken a few years after the fighting ended.

Just before dawn on December 21, 1866, the Sioux war chief Red Cloud mounted a snowy ridge some five miles north of the U.S. army outpost known as Fort Phil Kearny. The leader wore a thick buffalo robe draped over his shoulders; his face was lined and weathered, and his long black hair was braided and bound with strips of leather. Red Cloud had known many battles, yet today he was launching a campaign more ambitious than any he had ever ventured. Gravely weighing the dangers that lay before him, he watched his people move into position.

Below him, 2,000 Sioux, Cheyenne, and Arapaho warriors were bringing their horses to a halt on the ice-encrusted slopes of the Peno Valley. Carrying knives, clubs, bows, and rifles, their skin bright with war paint, they paused while Red Cloud's headmen issued their instructions. Red Cloud knew that the success of this battle depended on the Indians' ability to stay together and follow a carefully devised plan of action. They were to go boldly into combat, for they were fighting to protect their home and their people. They were not to content themselves with vain displays of bravery—they were to work quickly and destroy the enemy. Above all, they were not to rush into battle before the time had come for fighting, but to wait for a signal from their leaders.

It was precisely such disciplined action that would take the Indians' opponents, the U.S. troops stationed at Fort Phil Kearny, by surprise. The soldiers had been manning the fort—one of three ill-equipped army garrisons on the route from Nebraska to the western Montana gold mines—since August, when it was first completed. It was their job to defend the post as well as the miners and settlers who traveled past them toward Montana territory. Yet ever since they had first set foot in this region, Red Cloud's warriors had been attacking them almost without respite. Already the army had lost dozens of men and whole herds of horses and cattle. It had become impossible to protect the wagon trains that kept rolling doggedly into Sioux territory. There were simply too few troops and too many of Red Cloud's well-armed warriors.

All this notwithstanding, most of the men at Fort Phil Kearny looked down on their Indian enemies. Red Cloud might be able to lead an ambush, they reasoned, but he was, after all, uncivilized. He could never organize a large army or develop a coherent battle strategy. As far as the soldiers were concerned, it was just a matter of time before his whole force was annihilated.

The troops' commander, Colonel Henry B. Carrington, was not so self-assured. A skilled and well-educated administrator, he respected the Indians' fighting power and was disturbed by the knowledge that his forces were too small to match it. For months he had been pleading with his superiors to send more men, more arms, and more ammunition. The army, believing he was exaggerating the danger of his situation, had sent virtually nothing.

Meanwhile, the colonel's chief tactical officer, 25-year-old Captain William J. Fetterman, was certain that all Carrington needed to do was take the offensive and his troubles would quickly be over. Impatient with

Ambitious Civil War veteran Captain William Fetterman (pictured) was second in command at Fort Phil Kearny. Unlike his superior, Colonel Henry Carrington, Fetterman had little respect for the power of Red Cloud's warriors.

Carrington's command, he had been doing his best to turn the other officers against him, and to persuade them that the Indians' forces were negligible. "Give me 80 men," Fetterman was known to say, "and I will ride through the entire Sioux nation!"

Fetterman might have denied it, but Red Cloud's men had already come close to wiping out a quarter of the troops stationed at Fort Phil Kearny. On December 6, the Indians had ambushed a party of woodcutters west of the fort, and Carrington had sent Fettermen and 40 cavalrymen out to rescue them. Carrington himself had led a second 40-man detachment north toward Lodge Trail Ridge, where he hoped to entrap the warriors as they retreated. Yet before Fetterman could complete his maneuver, another Indian war party had spilled over the top of the ridge and assaulted Carrington's unit. The two officers had joined forces and, after vigorous combat, beat a retreat to Fort Phil Kearny. Two of their men had been killed and seven wounded, but it was clear that they had underestimated their enemy, and their losses could easily have been much higher. From that day on, Carrington had ordered his men to respond to all Indian attacks with extreme caution.

Red Cloud was confident that cold, clear December morning as he surveyed the Peno Valley. The night before, a Minneconjou prophet had received a sign that the Indians' campaign would be successful. Wearing a black cloth over his head and blowing a bone whistle, the mystic had ridden out from camp and disappeared over a nearby hill. When he returned a few minutes later, he approached Red Cloud and the other leading warriors, saying, "I have 10 men, 5 in each hand; do you want them?" The leaders shook their heads. He rode out again, this time swaying on his horse as he returned and announcing breathlessly, "I have 10 men in each hand.

Sioux, Cheyenne, and Arapaho warriors attack Fetterman's 80-man command near Peno Creek on December 21, 1866.

Twenty in all. Do you wish them?" Red Cloud and his men were still dissatisfied. On the third ride, the prophet returned with 50 men; still it was not enough. The Minneconjou rode out again, then galloped back, gasping. His horse stopped and he fell to the ground, striking the dirt with both hands. "Answer me quickly," he cried. "I have a hundred or more." Red Cloud and his fellow warriors shouted their approval. This omen, they knew, spelled victory.

As morning approached, the Indians had divided into three parties. While the main force deployed on either side of the Peno Valley, 10 of Red Cloud's most distinguished warriors gathered in a little gulley in the pine forest where Carrington's men cut their firewood. At the head of these warriors rode the brave and mysterious Sioux leader Crazy Horse, whose magical power, it was said, was so strong he could never be struck by an enemy. A third party was to make the initial attack on the woodcutters, whose distress signal would lure Carrington's men out from Fort Phil Kearny.

No sooner had the woodcutters come into view than the ambush party burst into action. Using mirror signals, Crazy Horse let Red Cloud know that the battle had begun.

At the sound of the woodcutters' three-shot alarm, Carrington's soldiers snapped to attention. The colonel had organized a relief force of 79 men for just this emergency, giving command of the unit to a cautious officer whose judgment he trusted. But as the men were about to go out, Fetterman rushed up and insisted that he himself be placed in command of the rescue party. The ambitious Fetterman was soon joined by Captain Fred Brown, who was scheduled to be transferred in a few days and wanted "one more chance to bring in the scalp of Red Cloud." Carrington reluctantly gave in to both officers, handing Fetterman a written order. "Support the wood train," read the colonel's instructions. "Relieve it and report to me. Do not engage or pursue Indians at its expense. Under no circumstances pursue over the ridge, that is, Lodge Trail Ridge." Carrington repeated these final words twice in person. Then he sent Fetterman out at the head of 80 soldiers—exactly the number he had said he would need to triumph over the Sioux.

The attack on the wood train broke off almost as soon as Fetterman left Fort Phil Kearny. But as the captain approached the scene of the battle, he spotted a small party of Indians hovering nearby. At the sight of the whites, the warriors scattered, whooping and yelling as they galloped away. Crazy Horse soon came charging back alone, shouting and waving his blanket as if to distract the troops from the warriors retreating behind him, then turned and raced back to join his party. Fetterman took the bait.

Zigzagging through the woods at a moderate pace so the soldiers could keep up, the Indians headed uphill toward Lodge Trail Ridge. From time to time, when the pursuit seemed to be lagging, they stopped altogether. Crazy Horse, who took up the rear, would dismount as if to cinch up his pony's war rope, check its hoof, or lead it for a stretch on foot. At one point he stopped and sat down to build a fire. When the other Indians gestured for him to drop what he was doing and follow, he motioned to them that his pony was lame, and they should go on without them. As bullets whizzed past his head, striking the trees and the snow around him, he watched his fellow warriors departing. Then, when Fetterman's troops were almost on top of him, he leaped onto his pony and raced after his companions, leading the soldiers over the top of Lodge Trail Ridge and down into the Peno Valley.

At a signal from Red Cloud, all 2,000 warriors burst out of hiding and attacked the soldiers from every side. "There were many bullets but there were more arrows," one Indian later remembered. "So many that it was like a cloud of grasshoppers all above and around the soldiers; and our people shooting across hit each other." Fetterman's men tried to scramble uphill, but the ice slowed them down; some ducked behind the few scattered boulders. The captain ordered his cavalry to head for the top of a slope, where there were more rocks to give them cover. Shouting their war cries, the Indians dashed through the shower of arrows to cut down the terrorized infantry. In less than 20 minutes they had finished with the foot soldiers and were crawling uphill toward the cavalry, using the rocks for shelter and moving ahead bit by bit until they were close enough to charge. With a whoop they descended on the last of Fetterman's men, swinging their axes and clubs with furious energy. Within 45 minutes, the entire detachment lay dead before them.

About an hour later, a relief force under Captain R. Ten Eyck rode out from the fort to find Fetterman. A party of Indians soon caught sight of them and tried to induce them to ride into the Peno Valley, but Ten Eyck kept his distance. Finally the Indians withdrew. They had won the day, and now a storm was coming, and it was time to take shelter. When Ten Eyck entered the valley, he found it strewn with stripped and mutilated bodies. Carrington described the Indians' work in his official report:

> Eyes torn out and laid on rocks; noses cut off; ears cut off; chins hewn off; teeth chopped out; joints of fingers, brains taken out and placed on rocks; entrails taken out and exposed; hands cut off, feet cut off; . . . eyes, ears, mouth,

and arms penetrated with spearhead, sticks, and arrows; . . . Punctures upon every sensitive part of the body, even to the soles of the feet and palms of the hand.

Miners, settlers, and soldiers all over the western plains were outraged by the so-called Fetterman massacre. General William T. Sherman, commander of the army's western division, proclaimed, "We must act with vindictive earnestness against the Sioux, even to their extermination, men, women, and children." Having lost just 13 men in the fighting, Red Cloud had managed a great triumph. His struggle, however, was just beginning.

2

A LAKOTA BOYHOOD

A pair of Sioux infants rest against a studio backdrop in this 19th-century photograph. As a baby, Red Cloud was kept in a cradleboard similar to those pictured here.

Red Cloud was born around 1822 near the confluence of the North Platte and South Platte rivers, in what is now western Nebraska. His mother, an Oglala Sioux named Walks As She Thinks, cared for him in the traditional Sioux manner, wrapping him in soft deerskin and securing him to a cradleboard so she could carry him on her back when she moved with her people or keep him propped against a nearby tree as she worked outdoors. Red Cloud's first home was a tipi—a cone-shaped tent constructed of long poles draped with buffalo hide—that his mother had set up near others of its kind on the broad Nebraska prairie. Historians believe that Red Cloud's father, a Brulé chief whose name was probably also Red Cloud, died soon after his son was born. After this, Walks As She Thinks went to live with her brother, Smoke, the leader of the Bad Face branch of the Oglala Sioux.

At the time of Red Cloud's birth, the Oglalas led a life of near-constant movement, camping in one area for only a few weeks at a time and then moving on, drifting back and forth across the plains west of the Missouri River. The Sioux had not always occupied this region. Their ancestors had lived farther east, in the present-day state of Minnesota, the name of which in fact comes from a Sioux word meaning "sky-colored water." In the fertile

Great Lakes area they had led a prosperous life, raising corn, beans, and squash, gathering roots, berries, and other edible plants, and hunting deer, elk, and buffalo. They had traded with their neighbors, the Arikaras and Mandans, who had a way of life similar to their own.

The Sioux—who called themselves the Lakotas, or "allies"—continued to inhabit Minnesota until around the middle of the 18th century, when the ever-expanding presence of European settlers in the east drove their traditional enemies, the Ojibwas, westward. After battling this tribe for several years, one branch of the Lakotas fled across the Missouri River, abandoning Minnesota for the Great Plains—the lands that would become North and South Dakota, Wyoming, Nebraska, and Colorado. This group became known as the Teton, or "prairie-dwelling" Sioux. Its seven subtribes—the Brulé, No-Bow, Two-Kettle, Minneconjou, Hunkpapa, Oglala, and Blackfoot Sioux—lived in separate encampments scattered across the plains, but they spoke the same language, shared the same culture, and would come together at times to hunt, feast, or fight against a common enemy.

On the vast midwestern prairies, crisscrossed by rivers and creeks bordered by cottonwoods, the Teton Sioux gave up agriculture and devoted their lives to pursuing the most prominent game in the area, the buffalo. They no longer stayed in permanent villages but set up temporary encampments wherever the hunting was favorable. Their possessions were few, and their tipis could easily be dismantled and carried as they followed the enormous herds that drifted across the plains.

Soon after moving west, the Teton Sioux made an acquisition that allowed their new nomadic mode of life to flourish: the horse. In their former home the Lakotas had always hunted and traveled on foot. On the plains, however, they came across not only large herds of wild ponies, descended from stock brought to North America by the Spanish, but also neighboring tribes who knew how to capture, tame, and ride them. After the Lakotas had mastered these skills, they were able to hunt, fight, and move camp with relative ease.

Indeed, the Lakotas' riding ability soon made them exceptional hunters and warriors, able to keep their families warm and well fed through the harsh midwestern winters, and capable of accumulating large herds of ponies through raids on enemy tribes. By the early 19th century, the Teton Sioux were among the wealthiest and most powerful Indians west of the Missouri River. George Catlin, an artist who spent years documenting the lives of Native Americans and who visited Lakota country in the early 1830s, wrote of the Indians,

> There is no tribe on the Continent, perhaps, of finer looking men than the Sioux; and few tribes who are better and more comfortably clad, and supplied with the necessaries of life. There are no parts of the great plains of America which are more abundantly stocked with buffaloes and wild horses, nor any people more bold in destroying the one for food, and appropriating the other to their use.

It was during this proud, dynamic period of Lakota history that Red Cloud came into the world.

Little is known about Red Cloud's early life, but it is likely that he grew up in the same loving atmosphere that surrounded most Sioux children. During his first few years he probably stayed near his mother, who looked after him with the help of other women in the Bad Face band as she worked tanning hides, sewing, or preparing her family's meals. When it was time for his people to move to a new encampment, Red Cloud could travel either on his mother's back or by travois—a vehicle formed of two poles with a hide stretched between them,

one end of which was harnessed to a horse while the other dragged along the ground. After Red Cloud learned to walk, he moved freely around the Bad Face encampment, where he enjoyed a great deal of attention—the whole Sioux community took part in the task of childrearing, and Red Cloud, like other children in his tribe, was no doubt encouraged to socialize and explore the world around him.

As he grew older, he may have joined other boys his age in a wide variety of games—activities that helped prepare him for a future as a hunter and warrior. Sioux boys, who learned to ride at an early age, held pony races and other competitions that tested their courage and agility on horseback. They took part in wrestling matches and mud-throwing contests, practiced shooting squirrels and other small game with miniature bows and arrows, and played a fast-paced ball game similar to present-day lacrosse.

As Red Cloud grew more adept at riding, shooting, and fighting, he probably looked forward to the day when he would join his first war party, riding with older members of the tribe against their enemies, the Crows and the Pawnees. The main goal of these intertribal campaigns was the capture of enemy horses. The Sioux warrior who took part in them could greatly enlarge his own pony herd—the main measure of his wealth. He could also gain enormous prestige. In the Sioux tradition, warfare was not only a matter of material gain but also an opportunity for a man to prove his strength, ingenuity, and courage. When a group of warriors returned from a campaign, the band would hold a dance to celebrate their achievements, during which each man told stories of his daring feats. Catlin, who called this custom the Dance of the Braves, described the way its participants earned the admiration of their people:

A Lakota warrior brandishes a lance in this drawing by George Catlin, an artist and ethnographer who visited the tribe in the early 1830s. "The personal appearance of these people is very fine and prepossessing," Catlin wrote, "their persons tall and straight, and their movements elastic and graceful."

At intervals they stop, and one of them steps in the ring, and vociferates as loud as possible, with the most significant gesticulations, the feats of bravery which he has performed during his life—he boasts of the scalps he has taken—of the enemies he has vanquished, and at the same time carries his body through all the motions and gestures, which have been used during these scenes when they were transacted. At the end of his boasting, all assent to the truth of his story, . . . and the dance again commences. At the next interval, another makes his boasts, and another, and another, and so on.

Young boys were often so eager to enter this circle of bold, proud warriors that they would steal away to join war parties without their parents' permission. Usually the leaders of the party would indulge these ambitious youths, allowing them to perform small tasks as the group approached an enemy camp but making sure they were protected when danger was close at hand. When a boy returned from such an outing, he would have his own stories—no doubt richly embellished—to tell his admiring peers.

The ability to tell such tales in a lively and convincing manner was almost as important as success on the battlefield, for speaking ability was one of the distinctions by which a young Lakota could rise to a position of leadership. It is said that Red Cloud possessed this gift at an early age—his eloquence would one day win him the loyalty of thousands of Lakota warriors.

Sometime during his early teens, Red Cloud joined his first adult hunting expedition and brought down his first buffalo. When he returned to camp with the kill, his uncle may have celebrated this important rite of passage by throwing a feast for the Bad Face band. Red Cloud's buffalo would have been butchered and each guest given a share of the meat along with an abundance of presents in honor of the boy's achievement.

Indian hunters close in on their prey in this Catlin painting. Lakota boys began learning to ride and shoot at an early age, for the buffalo hunt required great skill and endurance.

The Lakotas knew countless ways of preparing buffalo. The tongue, considered a delicacy, usually went to the hunter who made the kill. Sometimes the meat was cooked in a pouch made from the animal's stomach. It could also be dried and smoked into a kind of beef jerky. Pemmican, a food used while traveling or hunting, was a paste made up of meat and bone marrow mixed with berries.

The Lakotas used other parts of the buffalo to fulfill their need for clothing, shelter, and transportation. The women in the tribe tanned the hides and used them to construct everything from footwear to tipis to travois. Narrow strips of rawhide became rope, sinews became bowstrings, and bones were whittled into needles and other tools. Buffalo dung, after drying in the sun for several days, was burned as fuel. At the time of Red Cloud's youth, the Lakotas owed their survival to the buffalo, and they were well aware of their debt to this imposing creature. The buffalo played a central role in the Indians' spiritual life; Lakota hunters would offer a ritual apology to the buffalo before moving in for the kill.

Because horsemanship was an essential part of hunting and warfare among the Teton Sioux, a second milestone in the life of a Lakota boy was the capture of his first wild pony. Together with a team of older warriors, he would track a herd of ponies, then drive them across the prairie, sometimes for several days, until they were exhausted. Then he would select a horse, lasso it, pull it to the ground, hobble its forelegs, and allow it to struggle until it grew weak and compliant and could be ridden or led back to camp. George Catlin, who witnessed this procedure during his sojourn on the plains, was deeply impressed by the spectacle. "This 'breaking down' or taming," he wrote, "is not without the most desperate trial on the part of the horse, which rears and plunges in every possible way to effect its escape, until its power is exhausted, and it becomes covered with foam; and at last yields to the power of man, and becomes his willing slave for the rest of its life."

Once broken, the pinto ponies of the plains carried their masters with unparalleled speed, agility, and endurance. Although small in stature, they were strong and high-spirited. It was said that they could be ridden at a gallop for an entire day and all through the night without stopping. Taking full advantage of these qualities, Lakota warriors learned to maneuver their horses with precision and grace, to shoot with bow and arrow while riding at top speed, and to execute such stunts as sliding to one side of the horse and shooting from beneath its neck while using the animal as a shield against enemy fire. Red Cloud, who was to amass an especially large pony herd by the time he reached adulthood, quickly earned a reputation as a horseman of exceptional daring and talent.

At some point during his adolescence, Red Cloud may have gone through a ritual known as a vision quest, a spiritual exercise that was meant to provide Lakota boys with direction and guidance. A young man would prepare for the quest by fasting and purifying himself with a sweat bath in a special lodge made for this purpose. He was then left in a lonely spot, where he waited, naked and exposed to the elements. He neither ate nor drank for three or four days. At the end of this period, he often fell into a delirium, during which he might receive a sign revealing to him some aspect of his identity or his purpose in life.

One Lakota tradition maintains that Red Cloud held his vision quest in the Black Hills, where he sat and fasted for four days. After this period, he saw the clouds grow red, and then a scene that filled the landscape: many thousands of Lakotas and their allies, riding in formation. It was through this vision, according to some accounts, that Red Cloud received his first intimation of the great wars that would be fought when he reached adulthood, and of his future as the leader of one of the most powerful campaigns ever to be waged by Native American forces.

Some of Red Cloud's contemporaries also believed that the vision that came to him in the Black Hills was the source of his name. In the Lakota tradition, a boy was usually known by a nickname until he reached adolescence, when his people, acknowledging an important milestone in his life, such as his first buffalo hunt or his first battle, would give him his adult name. Sometimes a boy's vision served as inspiration for the name. The band might also name him after a relative, a phenomenon

A Lakota leader speaks at a tribal council. In the foreground, a warrior lights a pipe, a symbol of goodwill that will be passed from hand to hand throughout the meeting.

in nature, a personal characteristic, or an impressive accomplishment.

A number of Lakota accounts suggest that Red Cloud was named after his father. Red Cloud himself once confirmed this, tracing the name to the day he was invited to join his first war party. When he was 16 years old, he told an interviewer, one of his cousins was killed during a skirmish with the Pawnees, and the Oglalas organized a war party to avenge him. Red Cloud—who had not yet been given his adult name—was eager to join the campaign, but his mother was worried for his safety and tried to dissuade him. When the time came to depart and the young man had still not taken his place among the other warriors, a rumor spread that he had listened to his mother and that "his heart had failed him." The warriors laughed and started off without him. Before they could go far, however, a woman who had come to see them off announced that someone was coming. When they asked who it was, one warrior shouted, "Red Cloud's son!" Then, as the young warrior charged toward them on his pinto, fully decked in war paint and feathers, the welcoming cry was repeated by the group many times, until the words "Red Cloud's son!" became simply "Red Cloud!" In the ensuing battle with the Pawnees, the newly named Red Cloud took his first scalp, proving that he had truly become a man and a warrior.

Red Cloud's later exploits soon earned him a reputation as a bold and zealous fighter. In one pitched battle against the Pawnees, he reportedly killed four men with his own hands—an impressive accomplishment at a time when the loss of even one or two men was considered a brutal defeat for a tribe. During another raid, this time against the Crows, he made off with 50 horses in a single ambush, killing the Crow chief when the band pursued his party the next day.

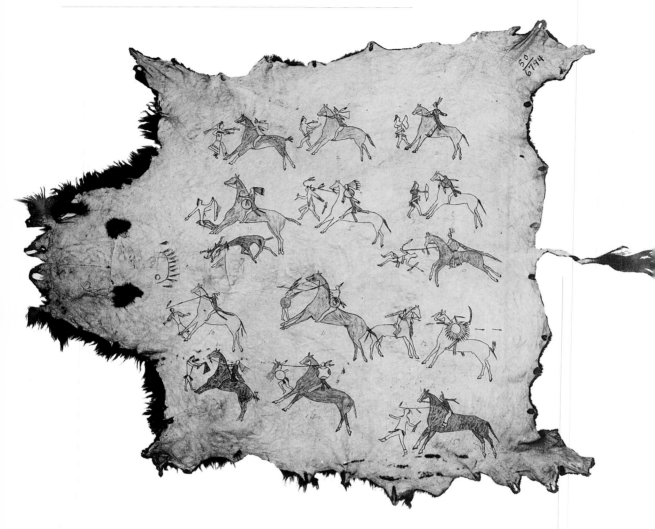

Some stories of Red Cloud's adventures on the battle-field suggest that—as his detractors would later claim—his character included a streak of cruelty. On one occasion, according to a contemporary named American Horse, the young warrior was fighting a campaign against the Utes when he spotted one of their warriors trying to cross a stream on a wounded horse. The horse stumbled, and the warrior fell in and was about to drown. Red Cloud rode out into the stream, grabbed the Ute by the hair, and

Battle scenes decorate this 19th-century Oglala buffalo robe. Warfare played an essential role in the life of the Lakotas, and it was Red Cloud's impressive fighting skills that first brought him fame and honor.

dragged him to safety. Then he drew his knife, scalped the man, and let his body fall to the ground.

As Red Cloud grew older, he continued to rehearse the arts of hunting, riding, and fighting—traditions that had been central to the life of the Teton Sioux for nearly a century. Meanwhile, all around him, events were taking place that would change this life forever.

3

"YOU HAVE SPLIT MY LAND"

Elaborately dressed in buckskins and feathers, the Oglala chief Bull Bear holds a metal ax, one of the tools the Indians acquired through trade. In 1841, Red Cloud killed Bull Bear in a dispute aggravated by alcohol, another trade item.

In the early 1800s, before Red Cloud was born, the Lakotas hunted and camped far to the west of the trading settlements of the Missouri River valley, and very few whites ever ventured onto their lands. But in the 1820s, fur traders began pushing into the heart of Lakota territory. Hoping to make their fortunes on buffalo and other animal hides, they established trading posts along the Platte River and competed with one another for the Indians' wares, luring them with offers of such manufactured goods as blankets, whiskey, guns, and metal implements. Many Indians coveted these items, which they could not obtain except through trade, and the posts soon became popular stopping places for the Lakotas, Cheyennes, Arapahos, and other plains tribes.

In 1834, when Red Cloud was about 12 years old, the Oglalas learned that traders had set up a post near the mouth of Laramie Creek on the North Platte River, in what is now eastern Wyoming, and were offering much sought after supplies to the Indians who came there. Before long the Bad Face Oglalas were camping close to this post, christened Fort Laramie, and dealing regularly with the traders who did business there.

35

Most of the items the Lakotas obtained at the post were tools that made their lives easier. Guns and ammunition, for example, made them more formidable hunters and warriors, and metal blades allowed them to cut wood, cure hides, and butcher game more efficiently. Yet one commodity brought them only hardship: alcohol. The Indians had not known liquor before the arrival of whites, and many traders tried to beat their competitors by taking advantage of the Indians' inexperience, first offering them whiskey as payment for their hides, then encouraging them to trade while under its influence and cheating them out of the goods they had earned.

After alcohol began circulating in the Lakota encampments, quarrels and rivalries flourished and sometimes flared into violence. Red Cloud not only witnessed such disturbances while the Bad Face band camped near Fort Laramie; in one dispute, he played a leading role. Even before the Oglalas began trading with the whites, bad feelings had existed between Red Cloud's uncle, Smoke, and a loud, aggressive chief named Bull Bear, the leader of the Koya band of the Oglalas. Tensions between the two chiefs increased when they moved near the fort and the domineering Bull Bear began to exert his power over all the Oglalas. The situation came to a head in the fall of 1841, when a young Bad Face warrior stole a woman from the Koyas. As news of this infringement spread through the Koya camp, Bull Bear, drunk on whiskey and bent on revenge, stormed over to the Bad Face encampment with a party of warriors. Without warning, the Koyas shot the father of the man who had taken the Koya woman and threatened to open fire on the entire Bad Face band. At that point a shower of arrows burst forth from the camp, and Red Cloud and a throng of young Bad Face warriors charged on the intruders. An arrow struck Bull Bear's leg and brought him to the ground;

Wielding a feathered lance, a Lakota horseman rides to battle in this 1850 woodcut.

Red Cloud rushed up and shot him through the head, killing him instantly. The Bad Face warriors then raced over to attack the Koya camp, but their rivals had fled; only a few women, children, and ponies remained, which the party took as spoils.

This incident left a breach between the Bad Face and Koya Oglalas that could not be healed. The Koyas found a new leader in Bull Bear's son, and eventually they drifted south to the lands between the Platte and Smoky

Hill rivers. Meanwhile, Red Cloud's part in the skirmish hastened his rise to leadership.

Soon after the death of Bull Bear, Red Cloud headed his first war party—one that would end in failure and almost cost the young leader his life. The campaign started out as a routine pony raid against the Pawnees, who were encamped south of the Platte on the Middle Loup River. Red Cloud and his men were to sweep down on the Pawnees, separate some of their horses from the main herd, and drive them back to the Oglala camp. But the Pawnees defended themselves with unexpected ferocity, and the Oglalas were forced to retreat without a single pony. After the chase, Red Cloud was found lying on the ground with an arrow protruding from his body. An older warrior withdrew the shaft and applied a poultice to the wound. By the next morning Red Cloud had revived enough to take food and water, and the Oglalas brought him back to camp by travois. For the next two months he lay on the brink of death. Finally, after a long convalescence, he regained his health, but the wound would continue to trouble him for the rest of his life.

Shortly after this episode, Red Cloud married a Lakota woman named Pretty Owl. Lakota men and women led very separate lives, and it is likely that the young warrior had little contact with his bride before marrying her. A man could court a young woman by meeting her in front of her tipi, where the two of them might stand close together enveloped in a buffalo robe. Once he decided to marry, he would offer a gift of ponies to the woman's father, who usually consulted his daughter before giving his consent. The marriage was sealed when the couple had slept together and the bride's parents had presented their new son-in-law with gifts in return for his offerings.

Lakota tradition allowed a man to take more than one wife, and this practice was especially common among tribal leaders. According to one historian, Red Cloud had intended to marry a woman named Pine Leaf about a month after his first marriage. But Pine Leaf was never told this, and she was so despondent over Red Cloud's marriage to Pretty Owl that she committed suicide on the night of their wedding. This incident left a deep impression on Red Cloud, who swore from then on he would remain monogamous. Whether he kept this promise has never been confirmed—one account actually places the number of his wives at six.

By the time Red Cloud had reached the end of his twenties, he was a well-respected warrior, renowned for his courage, passion, and drive. His people, meanwhile, had resolved none of the conflicts that had come with their involvement in trading. Disagreements over the proper way of dealing with the whites, as well as petty thefts and arguments inspired by the use of alcohol, continued to divide the Indians into factions. Some Lakotas were so impressed by the ease of living on trade goods that they gave up the freedom of the open plains and settled permanently near the fort, hunting only what they needed to continue trading. Those who remained true to Lakota tradition ridiculed these "Laramie Loafers," causing a rift in Lakota unity that was to burden the tribe for the next 40 years.

The Lakotas also faced a new set of worries. By the early 1840s, Fort Laramie had become a stopping place not only for traders but also for settlers headed for the fertile lands of the Far West. Traveling by horse, foot, and covered wagon, these emigrants, who at first passed through the Platte River valley in such small groups that they aroused only curiosity, came in ever larger and more threatening numbers as the decade progressed.

Whereas the traders had provided the Indians with useful tools and other supplies, this new group of whites

seemed to bring them only trouble. They cut down the cottonwoods that grew along the river; they allowed their horses and cattle to tear up and trample the prairie grass; they frightened away the buffalo with their gunfire and their long, rambling wagon trains. Although relations between the whites and the Indians began peacefully, in time the Indians displayed their resentment by harrassing the emigrants as they passed. The Oglalas, Brulés, and other Lakota bands would camp close to the Oregon Trail, as the emigrants' road was known, and demand that the settlers offer them food and other gifts in exchange for their safe passage. They made a sport of stealing the

Emigrants ford the North Platte River on their way to Fort Laramie and lands beyond in this 1842 painting by W. H. Jackson. As the number of settlers traveling through Lakota country expanded, the Indians' hostility increased.

settlers' cows, horses, and even such small items as pots and pans.

Soon enough, these raids came to the attention of the U.S. government. In the summer of 1845, Colonel Stephen W. Kearny and five companies of dragoons were sent to Lakota country to put a stop to them. Kearny held a council with the Bad Faces and other Oglalas on the Laramie River, where he paraded his troops in front of the Indians and warned them that if they harmed the emigrants they would be severely punished. The raids continued. Four years later the U.S. Army bought Fort Laramie from the American Fur Company and stationed a company of infantry there for the emigrants' protection.

That same year, an even more deadly blow struck the Indian encampments: smallpox, cholera, and measles—European diseases brought west by the emigrants, for which the Indians knew no cure. The Brulés and Oglalas tried to escape the epidemics by fleeing north to their traditional lands on the White River in South Dakota. There they encountered an entire village wiped out by cholera, its tipis all still standing, full of dead people. Sometime during this crisis, Red Cloud is said to have developed a remedy that helped his people survive. The medication, made from cedar leaves, was apparently used both as a drink and as an ointment for bathing.

By 1851 the epidemics had subsided, but the friction along the Oregon Trail had not. Some Indians regarded the illnesses they had recently endured as a form of magic used by the whites to destroy them, and their hostility toward the emigrants only grew stronger. Meanwhile, the Lakotas and other tribes continued to wage war against their Indian neighbors. Their actions frightened the settlers, who were never certain when they themselves would become the targets of such campaigns. The soldiers at Fort Laramie could do little to ease the settlers' anxieties, for their forces were too small to take direct action against the Indians.

Finally, U.S. officials followed a precedent they had set with tribes farther east: they decided to buy the settlers' right of way through Indian territory. Government agents and Indian runners traveled to camps all over the plains, calling the tribes to a council to be held at Fort Laramie in August 1851. The agents promised a great feast and gifts of beads, blankets, guns, and utensils to anyone who would come.

Some 10,000 Indians attended the meeting, including thousands of Lakotas, Cheyennes, and Arapahos, as well as the Lakotas' enemies the Shoshones and the Crows. Camped in a grassy valley near Fort Laramie, for nearly a month they feasted on government food and their own dogmeat—a dish for special occasions—while negotiating with the white authorities. At the end of this time a treaty was drawn up. In return for $50,000 a year for 50 years, the plains tribes were to allow the emigrants to pass unharmed along the Oregon Trail and the U.S. government to continue to build roads and forts in their territory. They were also to stop fighting one another and to recognize a plan, drawn up by the treaty commission, which divided the plains into separate territories for each tribe. Many of the Indians objected vigorously to these terms. "You have split my land and I don't like it," protested one Lakota leader. "These lands once belonged to the Kiowas and the Crows, but we whipped these nations out of them, and in this we did what the white men do when they want the lands of the Indians." Still, after much discussion, the commission secured enough signatures to declare the treaty valid. Although present at the meeting, neither Smoke nor any of the other Oglala leaders signed.

Buffalo meat hangs from a drying rack in this photograph of a plains Indian encampment. The picture was taken in 1853, the year the U.S. Army held its first council with the tribes trading at Fort Laramie.

At the Fort Laramie council, the commissioners also insisted that a head chief be appointed for each tribe so that the government could deal with a single leader in future negotiations. This idea was foreign to the Lakotas. The Bad Faces and other bands each had their own set of leaders, and even such powerful men as Smoke rarely acted as spokesmen for the others in his band, much less for the Teton Sioux as a whole. Lakota chiefs functioned primarily as advisers, role models, and strategists in war, their spheres of influence resting largely on their particular talents. The Lakotas were reluctant to select a head chief, so the commission appointed a Brulé leader named Conquering Bear, who had proved a cooperative man in trading.

To seal the decision, the commission organized a ceremony for Conquering Bear and the head chiefs of the Shoshones, Cheyennes, and Crows. The Indians assembled in a huge circle with the government agents in the center. With great formality, the head chiefs walked into the center, where the officials presented each with an officer's uniform. Pierre-Jean De Smet, a missionary who attended the meeting, described the spectacle: "Each was arrayed in a general's uniform, a gilt sword hanging at his side. Their long coarse hair floated above the military costume and the whole was crowned with the burlesque solemnity of their painted faces." Despite this demonstration, few Lakotas acknowledged Conquering Bear as their highest authority. Most of them simply ignored the new policy and continued with their own ways of governing.

When the council was over, the Oglalas headed north to hunt buffalo and to spend the winter near the Black Hills. In the spring they returned to Fort Laramie to trade, much as they had in previous years. The emigrants kept pouring across the plains; the Indians watched them warily, and when provocations arose, they continued to harrass them. Neither did the U.S. government uphold its end of the treaty. Before ratifying the agreement, the U.S. Senate unilaterally reduced the number of years the Indians would be paid from 50 to 15, cutting the total value of their reparations from $2.5 million to $750,000—less than $15 per person, according to some estimates. The summer of 1853 brought a brief skirmish between the Oglalas and U.S. troops in which a soldier, six Indians, and an emigrant family of four were killed. Much more blood would be spilled before it became clear to all that the Treaty of Fort Laramie was a failure.

4

THE BATTLE BEGINS

A tough veteran of the Mexican War, General William S. Harney swept into Lakota country in the fall of 1854, after a violent dispute between whites and Indians at Fort Laramie. Having wiped out some 80 Brulés at Blue Water Creek, Harney proclaimed the dawn of "a new era" in U.S.–Indian relations.

In August 1854, disaster struck the Platte River valley. That summer, as in previous years, the Bad Face Oglalas camped near Fort Laramie and waited for the government agent to bring them their yearly supply of blankets, tools, sugar, and coffee. They had set up their tipis near the camp of Conquering Bear's Brulés, not far from the Oregon Trail. One day a group of Mormons was passing along the trail when one of their cows wandered away and found its way into the Brulé camp. A Minneconjou warrior who was visiting at the time casually shot the cow, and the Indians butchered and ate it.

The owner, who had chased the cow to the edge of the camp but had been afraid to go farther, went straight to Lieutenant Hugh B. Fleming, the commander at Fort Laramie, and told him the animal had been stolen. To Fleming's men, bored and restless after a long, hot summer far from civilization, this misdeed looked like an excuse for action.

The commander summoned Conquering Bear to the fort and demanded that he turn in the Minneconjou. The Lakota chief—who felt he had no authority over warriors from other bands—offered to compensate the owner of the cow instead. This offer was not enough for Fleming, who had taken it into his head to chasten the offender.

47

The next day he sent a brash, heavy-drinking, 24-year-old lieutenant named John L. Grattan and 29 soldiers to the Brulé camp to arrest the Minneconjou. Meanwhile, both the Oglalas and the Brulés conferred with Conquering Bear and—not knowing where the soldiers' action would lead—prepared for war. The warriors were waiting behind a bluff when the troops arrived.

Grattan rode straight up to Conquering Bear and ordered him to produce the warrior who had killed the cow. The Minneconjou resisted, and Conquering Bear refused to force him. Grattan and the Brulé chief parleyed for half an hour. Then Grattan abruptly broke off the talks and ordered his men to open fire on the Indians. After the first volley, Conquering Bear fell dead with nine bullets in his body. In an instant the warriors poured over the ridge, released a barrage of arrows, and wiped out Grattan and every one of his men.

That night the Indians stormed the post of a French trader and spoke of attacking Fort Laramie itself, where their annuity goods were stored. Before they could agree on a plan, however, they discovered that the women had packed up the tipis and were preparing to escape north. The men, whose first duty was to keep their families safe, decided to follow. For the next several months, the Oglalas and Brulés stayed well away from the Platte River, hunting buffalo.

Yet the Lakotas had forgotten neither the loss of Conquering Bear nor the success of their first serious battle with U.S. forces. In November, a Brulé leader named Spotted Tail and four of his warriors picked up where their tribesmen had left off and attacked a mail wagon traveling on the Oregon Trail, killing two drivers and a passenger and stealing $20,000 in cash. The following spring, a party of Brulés, Minneconjous, and Oglalas launched a whole series of sporadic attacks, sweeping down on wagon trains and driving off horses and cattle all along the Platte River. Some historians believe that Red Cloud played a leading role in this intermittent campaign.

A few months later came the whites' reprisal. In the summer of 1855, the U.S. War Department ordered General William S. Harney, a hero of the Mexican War, to assemble a force of 600 men at Fort Leavenworth in eastern Kansas in preparation for a punitive drive against the Sioux. The new government agent at Fort Laramie, Thomas S. Twiss, sent messengers out to all the Lakota bands, warning them that any Indians who did not move south to the Platte River that fall would be hunted down by Harney's forces. More than half the bands, including the Oglalas, were intimidated by the agent's words, and quickly gathered near Fort Laramie.

Harney intended to discipline the rest by cutting across the plains northeast of Fort Laramie—where the Oglalas and Brulés did most of their hunting—and attacking all the Indians in his path. About 100 miles east of the fort, on the Bluewater River, he came across his first target: a band of Brulés who had just completed a buffalo hunt and were preparing the meat and hides for the winter. Little Thunder, the leader of the group, had made no plans for protecting his people. Harney sent his cavalry over the hills to the far end of the camp and entered from the front with his infantry and artillery. Little Thunder came out to meet him, and the two held council long enough for Harney's troops to get into position. When Harney gave the order to charge, the Brulés could do nothing but race for the hills—and into the attacking cavalry. Within 30 minutes the soldiers had killed 86 Indians and captured 70 women and children. Fewer than 100 escaped to wander the plains without food or shelter.

After marching his prisoners to Fort Laramie, Harney set out across the plains again, headed for Fort Pierre on the Missouri River. On the way, he met not a single Indian, so awed were the Sioux by the enormous power of the white army. The Lakotas had never known such a massive defeat as the Bluewater Creek "rubout." In all their battles against the Crows and the Pawnees, they had rarely come away with more than one or two casualties. Neither had they ever attempted to wipe out their enemies before their attack on Grattan and his men at Fort Laramie. The usual Sioux practice was to come away from a battle with impressive spoils and stories of one's fighting skill and courage. Touching an enemy warrior with a hand or a coup stick—a richly decorated staff made especially for this purpose—brought a warrior almost as much honor as scalps or other trophies proving the death of an opponent. Stunned by their enormous losses, for the next several months the Lakotas offered the U.S. Army no resistance.

In March 1856, Harney held a council at Fort Pierre and persuaded most of the Lakota chiefs to sign another treaty confirming the terms of the 1851 agreement. After this meeting, the Brulés, Oglalas, and other Lakota tribes retreated to the northern plains, where the whites were far away and the buffalo were plentiful. Once a year they journeyed to Fort Laramie to collect their annuities.

The Indians had become more cautious, but they were hardly ready to relinquish their territory, either to the settlers, who had already succeeded in driving the buffalo from the Platte River valley, or to the U.S. military, who had begun to police Lakota lands. In the summer of 1857, the leaders who had attended Harney's meeting invited all the tribes of the Teton Sioux to a grand council at Bear Butte, just north of the Black Hills, where they

Assisted by Chinese immigrants, gold miners sift through the sand in a California creek bed. In the early 1860s, prospectors discovered gold in Montana, some 300 miles west of the Lakotas' prime hunting grounds.

would decide on a common policy for dealing with the whites.

More than 5,000 Sioux gathered at the base of Bear Butte that August. Red Cloud, who was by this time in his thirties and widely known as one of the Lakotas' most fearsome warriors, attended the meeting alongside such illustrious leaders as the Hunkpapa warrior and healer Sitting Bull, Crow Feathers of the No-Bows, and Long Mandan of the Two-Kettles. Among the Oglalas were

16-year-old Crazy Horse, who was to become one of the century's most celebrated warriors, along with the chief of his band, Red Cloud's longtime friend Man Afraid of His Horse. After long discussion, these men and the rest of the council participants pledged to work together to prevent further white encroachments on their lands. They made no provision for confronting an army that, as they had seen already, was so large and well equipped that it could easily overwhelm them. Their only strategy was a determination to fight.

After the Great Teton Council, the Oglalas headed for the plains west of the Black Hills, where the Crows and Shoshones had their hunting grounds. Finding the area rich in buffalo, they continued to camp there for the next several years, avoiding the whites in the Platte River valley and waging war instead on their traditional Indian enemies. By the early 1860s, the Oglalas had taken control of most of the Powder River valley and were hunting almost exclusively in this region. Surrounded by buffalo and far from the influences of the U.S. Army, which was by this time involved in the Civil War, Red Cloud and his people enjoyed a period of prosperity.

It would not be long, however, before the Oglalas' new lands began to slip away from them. By 1861, the first miners had already passed through the Powder River valley and discovered gold in the mountains of western Montana Territory. From that point on, ambitious prospectors continued to cross the northern plains, following a trail that ran northwest from Fort Laramie toward the Yellowstone River and beyond it to the mining settlements of Helena and Virginia City.

More signs of trouble came in 1862, when long-standing conflicts between Minnesota settlers and the Oglalas' eastern relatives, the Santee Sioux, led to a bloody rebellion. After the Santee uprising, in which as many as

Minnesota settlers rest during their flight from the Santee Sioux in 1862. Following years of tension between Indians and whites in the Great Lakes region, the Santee uprising led to the death of as many as 750 settlers.

750 settlers were killed, the U.S. Army stormed Minnesota and took most of the tribe prisoner. Thirty-eight of the Santees were hanged before the citizens of Mankata, Minnesota, in the largest execution in U.S. history.

In the wake of this crisis, many of the Santees fled west and took shelter among the Tetons. The U.S. Army followed them, determined to punish not only the Santees but any Indians who crossed their path. In the summer of 1863, U.S. troops under General Henry Sibley fought a combined force of Santees and Hunkpapas at Dead Buffalo and Stony lakes in present-day North Dakota. The following year, a second U.S. regiment attacked a camp of eastern and western Sioux between the Heart and Little Missouri rivers, about 250 miles northeast of the Oglalas' hunting grounds. Meanwhile, news of the Santee uprising aroused fear and hostility among settlers and miners all across the western plains.

Throughout the summer of 1864, as government troops marched toward the frontier, violence flared along the Platte River and in the mining towns of Colorado. In August, Colorado governor John Evans issued a proclamation urging settlers to band together and hunt down Indians. He was supported by the territory's military commander, Colonel John M. Chivington, who gathered a regiment of more than 600 volunteers and set out to fulfill the governor's order.

In November, Chivington came across a band of Cheyennes camped at Sand Creek, near Fort Lyon. Their chief, Black Kettle, was a man of peace, and he was staying near the fort because the commanding officer there had agreed to grant him protection. Chivington did not care. "I have come to kill Indians," he announced, "and believe it is right and honorable to use any means . . . to kill Indians." At dawn on November 27, Chivington and his men surrounded the camp and opened fire. As women and children fell dead around them, the Cheyenne warriors fought back desperately, but the odds were heavily against them. By the end of the battle, the volunteers had killed more than 130 Cheyennes. They tracked down and beat to death escaping families, scalped them, and mutilated their bodies. Only nine of Chivington's men were killed.

Most Americans greeted the news of the massacre with horror. The frontiersman Kit Carson called it "the action of a coward and a dog." Chivington was eventually forced to resign his commission, and a committee was established to try to negotiate peace in the region.

Colonel John M. Chivington, the boastful, arrogant commander of a hastily enlisted regiment of Colorado volunteers, slaughtered a peaceful band of Cheyennes in November 1864. Known as the Sand Creek massacre, Chivington's assault inspired the Lakotas, Cheyennes, and Arapahos to prepare for war.

The damage, however, was already done. News of the massacre quickly spread north to the Oglalas and other Sioux bands, and the Cheyennes sent with it their war pipes. There was to be no more talk of appeasing the whites or cooperating with the U.S. government. Black Kettle had advocated peace, and the whites had destroyed him. Now it was time for war.

That winter, the Cheyennes and their allies plundered white settlements up and down the South Platte River, tearing down telephone poles, raiding wagon trains, and attacking army posts and stagecoach stations. Red Cloud, Crazy Horse, and other Oglalas rode south from the Powder River to join the fighting, and in January the united Indian forces sacked the town of Julesburg. Then, leaving a trail of devastation behind them, the entire party swept back through the bitter cold to their northern hunting grounds, where they celebrated their victories.

In May 1865, more than 8,000 Cheyennes, Sioux, and Arapahos gathered to discuss their next campaign. Red Cloud, who led the council along with his friend Man Afraid of His Horse, stirred the passions of his fellow warriors with his fervent oratory, telling them:

> The Great Spirit raised both the white man and the Indian. I think he raised the Indian first. He raised me in this land and it belongs to me. The white man was raised over the water and his land is over there. Since they crossed the sea, I have given them room. There are now white people all about me. I have but a small spot of land left. The Great Spirit told me to keep it.

At the end of June, the Indians prepared for a full-scale offensive against the whites. For days they consulted their medicine men, seeking an omen that might guide them during the hard battles ahead. They painted their bodies, decorated their horses, practiced war songs, and put their weapons in order. In July the great war party—some 3,000 warriors in all—struck camp and headed out in a wide column, with Red Cloud, his friend's son Young Man Afraid of His Horse, and the Cheyenne chief Roman Nose in the lead. This was the largest war party the plains Indians had ever assembled, and their numbers made them bold.

On July 24, they reached the hills above Platte Bridge Station, a U.S. military post west of Fort Laramie. The Indians planned to attack the fort using a decoy technique, first drawing the soldiers out into the open and then surprising them with their superior forces. On July 25, 20 warriors, including the illustrious Crazy Horse, rode down toward the bridge and paraded back and forth in front of the garrison, motioning to the corral on the opposite bank as though planning to steal the army's horses. A company of troops rushed out of the fort and raced across the bridge, a howitzer—a short cannon—in tow. But on the north bank the soldiers stopped and would go no farther. Finally the Indians fired a few shots at the troops, who responded with some blasts from the howitzer. The noise of gunfire so tantalized the eager warriors waiting behind the hills that, without waiting for a signal, they rushed to the top of a ridge to see what was happening, and the frightened soldiers retreated.

The leaders of the campaign were angered by this blunder, but the next day they fared better. They had repeated their tricks for several hours without success when a party of cavalry poured out of the stockade to protect the nearby Oregon Trail, where a wagon train was approaching. The warriors attacked first the cavalry and then the wagon train, killing eight soldiers and most of the emigrant drivers. After this minor victory, the Indians held a scalp dance and then headed back to the Powder River.

The Brulé chief Spotted Tail became convinced of the overwhelming power of the U.S. government during his imprisonment by Harney in the late 1850s. After his release, officials generally regarded him as one of the "friendly" Sioux.

That same summer, the U.S. government, determined to take control of the western regions once and for all, sent three columns of troops into northern Lakota country. After tracking down and subduing the Sioux, these men were to establish posts along the Bozeman Trail, the main road leading from Fort Laramie to the Montana mining settlements. Poorly trained and ill at ease in the Wyoming wilderness, the troops failed in both endeavors. They managed to attack a few small bands of Sioux but scored no conclusive victories, and otherwise wandered chaotically around with little sense of purpose.

In the fall of 1865, a company led by Colonel Patrick Connor built a fort near the source of the Powder River, later to be known as Fort Reno. In the winter, Red Cloud and his followers laid siege to the fort, cutting off the soldiers' supply lines. By February half the soldiers were suffering from malnutrition or pneumonia. By ones and twos, the troops deserted.

Even as this military campaign was taking its disastrous course, the Indian Bureau in Washington, D.C., was putting together a new treaty commission in hopes that the tribes could be negotiated with peacefully. The commission went first to the "friendly" bands that continued to camp near Fort Laramie and other government posts. By the fall of 1865 no fewer than nine bands of Sioux had agreed to guarantee whites the use of the Bozeman Trail. Yet none of these bands lived anywhere near the Powder River, nor did they make their living hunting. Indeed, the life of these "Loafers-About-the-Fort" was by now vastly different from that of the northern Sioux, and their readiness to give up the Powder River region—a land most of them had never visited—had little meaning. Realizing they had to secure at least a few signatures from the north, the commissioners sent runners to the Powder River requesting that the "hostile" leaders come to Fort Laramie for another council.

In the spring of 1866, the Brulé chief Spotted Tail answered the commissioners' summons. Spotted Tail's daughter, Fleet Foot, was very ill, and he may have hoped to get treatment for her at Fort Laramie. By the time he arrived, Fleet Foot had died. Moved by the leader's grief and recognizing an opportunity to win his friendship, Colonel Henry Maynadier, the commanding officer, held a funeral for her near the post. Spotted Tail wept openly, and from this point on, Maynadier felt that the Brulé's cooperation was assured.

Soon after this, Red Cloud and Man Afraid of His Horse arrived at Fort Laramie with some 200 of their people. There they received a telegram that read:

The Great Father in Washington has appointed the commissioners to treat with the Sioux, the Arapahos and Cheyennes . . . on the subject of peace. He wants you all to be his friends and friends of the white man. If you conclude a treaty of peace, he wishes to make presents to you and your people as a token of friendship.

Spotted Tail's daughter Fleet Foot, who died shortly before the 1866 Fort Laramie council, was laid to rest on this scaffold. The officer who arranged for her funeral was rewarded with Spotted Tail's cooperation throughout the meeting.

The council convened at the end of May. Red Cloud and the other leaders who had come to the meeting seemed ready to negotiate peace. Yet for many days, the main purpose of the new treaty—to obtain right-of-way for travelers on the Bozeman Trail—was never mentioned. Meanwhile, the president ordered Colonel Henry Carrington to take a new set of troops into the area and to build more posts for the whites' protection. The army's timing was unfortunate. On June 13, only a few days after the commission first brought up the matter of the

Bozeman Trail, Carrington's regiment arrived from the east outside the gates of Fort Laramie.

Red Cloud, who quickly caught wind of the army's intentions, bristled with indignation. "The Great Father sends us presents and wants us to sell him the road," he told the commission. "But the White Chief [Carrington] goes with soldiers to steal the road before the Indians say yes or no!"

Then, according to an account by Sergeant Sam Gibson, a member of Carrington's company, "Red Cloud . . . grabbed his rifle and shook it in the faces of the Commissioners, declaring that the soldiers should not pass through his favorite hunting grounds, and that he would kill every soldier and wage a war of extermination against all white invaders." The Oglala leader stormed from the meeting place, mounted his horse, and galloped away with all 200 of his warriors.

5

RED CLOUD'S WAR

Red Cloud's departure from the council of 1866 abruptly ended all genuine negotiation between the Lakotas and the U.S. government. Yet the treaty commissioners simply gathered more signatures from the "friendly" chiefs and wired news of their success to Washington. "Satisfactory treaty concluded with the Sioux," read their telegram. "Most cordial feeling prevails." Red Cloud, meanwhile, was traveling all over the northern plains, passing the war pipe among the Oglalas, Minneconjous, Hunkpapas, No-Bows, Brulés, northern Cheyennes, and Arapahos and trying to persuade them to join him in an all-out offensive against the whites. He even went to his enemies, the Crows, and asked them to put aside their grievances to help defend Indian lands from white intruders. The Crows turned him down, but many others were eager to follow the ambitious Oglala leader.

On June 16, Carrington and his men left Fort Laramie and began making their way north along the Bozeman Trail. Lakota scouts followed their every movement. Red Cloud's men made their first full-scale raid in early July, sweeping down from the hills toward the army's pack animals and driving off almost 200 head of livestock before retreating. Carrington's men pursued them, only to find themselves attacked from the flank by another

This photograph, taken in 1870, is the earliest known image of Red Cloud. The Oglala leader amassed a force of 2,000 warriors to defend the Powder River valley from white intrusion. Known as Red Cloud's War, his campaign was one of the most effective in northern plains history.

party of warriors. Several soldiers were killed, and Red Cloud withdrew with minimal losses.

From that point on, the Indians kept up a near-constant pattern of harassment: horses were stampeded, soldiers picked off, messengers intercepted. After exploring more than 60 miles of wilderness under these harrowing conditions, the colonel finally selected the site for his headquarters near Piney Creek, about halfway between the Powder and Bighorn rivers.

The troops quickly set to work building a fort, but it was not easy, for Red Cloud had as many as 4,000 warriors under his command, and he had no intention of letting Carrington rest for even a moment. The nearest suitable wood was seven miles away from the construction site, and the wood-gathering parties were frequently ambushed and had to be rescued by the others. When the rescue parties went out, a second party of warriors would attack the soldiers' camp and stampede their horses and pack mules. By the end of the summer, according to one report, the army had lost its entire stock of cattle.

Still, by the fall, the fort was completed. Carrington named it Fort Phil Kearny, after a general of the recently ended Civil War. Built on a high plateau overlooking the Bozeman Trail, the stoutly constructed pine stockade was as close to impregnable as the army's engineers could make it. From within the fort, Carrington wrote his superiors, he could stand off a thousand attackers, provided he had enough ammunition.

Carrington soon sent a detachment of infantry north to establish a second post, Fort C. F. Smith, on the Bighorn River. This left as few as 350 men to defend Fort Phil Kearny and guard a 100-mile stretch of the Bozeman Trail. The soldiers' task was impossible. They could hardly travel more than a few hundred yards from the fort without inviting an Indian attack. Hunting and

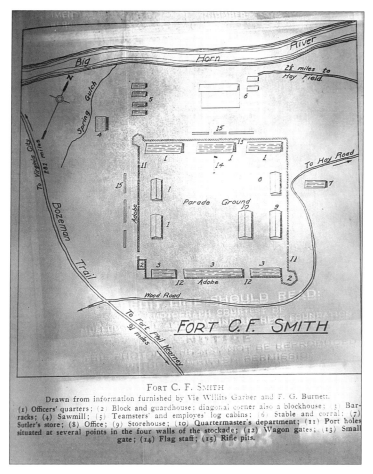

FORT C. F. SMITH
Drawn from information furnished by Vie Willits Garber and F. G. Burnett.
(1) Officers' quarters; (2) Block and guardhouse: diagonal corner also a blockhouse; (3) Barracks; (4) Sawmill; (5) Teamsters' and employes' log cabins; (6) Stable and corral; (7) Sutler's store; (8) Office; (9) Storehouse; (10) Quartermaster's department; (11) Port holes situated at several points in the four walls of the stockade; (12) Wagon gates; (13) Small gate; (14) Flag staff; (15) Rifle pits.

This sketch shows the layout of Fort C. F. Smith, built by Carrington's men soon after they completed Fort Phil Kearny. Red Cloud's warriors made frequent attacks on the army's stable and corral (6) and the trader's store (7).

woodcutting parties needed armed escorts, and some never returned.

Soon after the establishment of Fort Phil Kearny, Red Cloud had set up his own base camp some miles away on the upper Powder River. From there parties of warriors went out every day to attack the fort and the wagon trains that passed along the Bozeman Trail. While some men participated in the raiding, others rested and regained their strength or went hunting to keep the camp supplied with buffalo. Although Red Cloud's warriors never acted as a unified army in the first few months of fighting, their campaign was effective. Between August and December 1866, they killed 154 soldiers and travelers, captured nearly 700 horses, cattle, and mules, and mounted 51 direct attacks on Fort Phil Kearny. The Indians rarely let a group of travelers pass through the country unmolested. Sometimes, reported Sergeant Sam Gibson, they would encircle a train and keep it "corralled three or four days between watering places, so that men and animals suffered extremely from thirst."

This string of triumphs was due largely to Red Cloud's gifts as an organizer, adviser, and strategist. Having reached the age of 45, he took a less active role in the fighting than the younger warriors, but for those who did engage in combat, he remained a constant source of direction and inspiration. By maintaining ties with some of the "friendly" Brulés camped farther south, he was able to organize regular trading runs between Fort Laramie and his encampment and to keep his followers well stocked with food, weapons, and ammunition. He was also an able military adviser. By the mid-1860s, according to Lakota sources, Red Cloud had counted 80 coups. His long experience, fierce ambition, and powerful personality helped sustain his warriors through the longest and most cohesive campaign they had ever waged.

After Red Cloud's successful campaign against Captain William Fetterman, the Indians may have believed that a final victory was close at hand. They maintained their siege of Fort Phil Kearny throughout the winter, and by the spring of 1867, they had stopped all traffic along the Bozeman Trail. As spring turned to summer, Red Cloud and his followers met once more in council. It was time for a decisive blow. As their talks progressed, however, it became clear that Red Cloud and the Cheyenne war chiefs Dull Knife and Two Moon had different ideas about what that blow should be. The

Cheyennes wanted to attack Fort C. F. Smith, where raiders had killed or stolen almost all of the cavalry's horses. Red Cloud preferred to finish the job he had started and destroy Fort Phil Kearny. Unable to reach an agreement, the war party split up. In August, Dull Knife went north to lead an attack on Fort C. F. Smith, while Red Cloud drew up plans for the devastation of Fort Phil Kearny.

The Cheyennes lost more than 20 men in their fight at Fort C. F. Smith. Red Cloud fared even worse. Once again, a small party of warriors was sent out to attack a wood train near Fort Phil Kearny with the aim of drawing Carrington's soldiers out into the open. But this time the trick misfired: the second war party attacked prematurely, spoiling the warriors' chances of taking the troops by surprise. Determined to save the campaign, Red Cloud's second-in-command, Hump, directed his warriors to attack the wood train in earnest.

The wood train was guarded by a detachment of soldiers under Captain James W. Powell. When setting up camp, these men had removed the wheels from 14 wagon boxes and arranged them in a circle to make a corral for their horses and mules. When the Indians attacked, the whites quickly took cover in the boxes. Red Cloud's warriors attacked the soldiers using their standard technique: they circled the corral, riding just close enough to to draw the whites' fire, then closed in to do their own shooting while their enemies reloaded.

But the soldiers did not stop firing. As it turned out, Carrington's men had recently been issued a new set of Springfield repeating rifles, which could fire eight times before they needed to be reloaded. The Indians rode directly into the whites' second volley. They rode forward again, only to be fired on once more. Finally they left their horses behind them and tried charging on foot. But

no matter how they approached the wagon boxes, a warrior named Fire Thunder later related, "It was like green grass withering in a fire." Finally the Indians picked up their wounded and withdrew.

The so-called Wagon Box Fight marked a major defeat for the Indians. Yet despite appearances, Red Cloud was winning his war. In a single year, the campaign against the Bozeman Trail had brought the government enormous losses in men and materials. Meanwhile, the army was more urgently needed in the Platte River valley,

Man Afraid of His Horse smokes a council pipe during a May 1868 meeting at Fort Laramie. Red Cloud refused to enter negotiations with the government until the following November.

where the Kansas Pacific Railroad was under construction. As early as the spring of 1867, the U.S. government had sent a new peace commission to Fort Laramie, and throughout the summer, these men had tried to attract Red Cloud and other Indian leaders to a new treaty council. By the fall, General Sherman had joined the commission and set out to negotiate a treaty with Red Cloud as soon as possible—he was prepared to give the Indians generous terms.

On November 9, the peace commission arrived at Fort Laramie, where Sherman had hoped to hold a grand council with the Sioux. He was greeted only by Man Afraid of His Horse, who told them that Red Cloud and his warriors were fighting to protect the last of their hunting grounds, and that they refused to stop until the army abandoned all its forts on the Bozeman Trail. Sherman balked at this, for he knew that to the soldiers who had been risking their lives to defend the forts for the past two years, such a capitulation would be deeply demoralizing. The council dissolved.

Throughout the following winter, Red Cloud's warriors continued to obstruct travel on the Bozeman Trail. Although they mounted no more direct attacks on the forts, they kept the soldiers constantly on the defensive. By the spring, Sherman had decided to let Red Cloud have his way.

On March 2, 1868, President Ulysses Grant ordered the army to abandon Forts Reno, C. F. Smith, and Phil Kearny. Yet another peace commission assembled, and a new treaty was drawn up. It promised that the Lakotas could keep forever all of the western half of South Dakota, and that they could continue to hunt in the "unceded Indian territory" from the Black Hills to the Bighorn Mountains. The army promised to abandon its posts in this region, and no more whites were to trespass there.

The agreement was to remain valid "as long as the grass will grow, as long as the rivers will flow and as long as the dead lie buried."

The commissioners arrived at Fort Laramie that April, hoping to find Red Cloud ready to meet with them. The Oglala war chief, however, took his time. As the treaty circulated among the "friendly" Sioux, Red Cloud and his followers kept watch on the Bozeman forts, waiting for the whites to keep their promise. On July 29, 1868, the troops marched out of Fort C. F. Smith. The next morning, Red Cloud's warriors burned it to the ground. A few days later, the same thing happened at Forts Reno and Phil Kearny.

In August, Red Cloud sent word to Fort Laramie that he would come in to talk when he had finished preparing his meat from a recent buffalo hunt. Not until November 4 did he join some 125 Oglala, Hunkpapa, No-Bow, and

Lakota Indians gather outside Fort Laramie during the council of 1868. Red Cloud's War ended on November 4, when the Oglala leader signed a treaty in which the U.S. government relinquished its rights to the Bozeman Trail.

other Lakota leaders attending the Fort Laramie council. Two days later, "with a show of reluctance and tremulousness [he] washed his hands with the dust of the floor" and made his mark on the treaty.

Red Cloud had achieved something no other Indian had: through the sheer strength of his fighting power, he had forced the United States to bow to his demands. Yet the Treaty of 1868 also made some demands of its own, many of which Red Cloud may not have fully understood. Although the Lakotas were to be allowed to hunt freely in the lands near the Powder River, they were to make their permanent homes near the government agencies that would soon be established on their reservation in western South Dakota. At the agencies they would receive goods and services that would enable them to lead the "civilized" life favored by the whites. The Indians would be taught to farm, and each agency would provide them with basic foods as well as the services of a doctor, a blacksmith, a carpenter, an engineer, and a miller for at least 10 years. Although the commissioners may have considered this arrangement a more humane approach to the Indian problem than the policy of subduing the tribes through war, Red Cloud and his followers were to find in it the source of a long series of hardships.

6

▼ ▼ ▼

"ALL I WANT IS RIGHT AND JUST"

Caught between the old life and the new, Red Cloud wears a buckskin jacket fringed with ponytails and holds a cane in this 1880 studio photograph.

After the Fort Laramie council, Red Cloud returned to the Powder River to camp with Crazy Horse, Man Afraid of His Horse, and the rest of the northern Oglalas. The Indians spent the winter hunting buffalo and enjoying their newly won freedom. Game was scarce that season, however, and in the spring Red Cloud returned to Fort Laramie, where he hoped to obtain rations for some 1,000 of his followers. Some six months after he had signed the Treaty of 1868, Red Cloud discovered one of its least attractive provisions. As the Fort Laramie agent soon informed him, the Oglalas now had an agency at Fort Randall, some 300 miles to the east on the Missouri River, and it was at this post that they were to collect their annuities and do all their trading.

Red Cloud had no interest in traveling to Fort Randall. It was far from the Lakotas' usual hunting ground, there was no game near the post, and at the 1868 council he had insisted repeatedly that he be allowed to continue trading at Fort Laramie. After a long discussion and a volley of telegrams to Washington, the agent gave Red Cloud some provisions and sent him on his way. When Red Cloud returned to Fort Laramie that fall, he was

73

Members of a Lakota family rest outside their tipi in a village supplied with government-issued blankets, wagons, and meat. Throughout the early 1870s, Red Cloud petitioned the U.S. government for permission to obtain such goods at his traditional trading post, Fort Laramie, rather than at the post he had been assigned on the Missouri River.

again ordered to move to Fort Randall. Again Red Cloud refused.

Unsure how to resolve this conflict, Washington officials decided to try a strategy they had already employed with many other Indian leaders. They invited Red Cloud to the capital to meet with the Great White Father, the president.

On May 26, Red Cloud boarded the Union Pacific Railroad with 20 friends and advisers. They arrived in Washington about a week later. Red Cloud was surprised to learn that Spotted Tail, with whom he had been at odds since the council of 1866, was also in Washington. The Brulé leader was unhappy with his new home on the Missouri and, like Red Cloud, wanted to return to his old encampment near Fort Laramie.

Over the next few days, the Oglalas toured the capital and the nearby navy yards. They met U.S. officials, saw the whole city stretched out before them from the Capitol dome, and watched Congress debate an Indian appropriation bill from the Senate gallery. They were shown huge cannons and ironclad battle ships and taken to lavish theater entertainments.

If the goal of the trip was to intimidate the Indians, it did not succeed. Red Cloud did not appear dazzled by the power and wealth of the U.S. government, nor was he frightened by a huge cannon in the navy yards that threw shells 5 miles downriver. (It took a very long time to move and aim the gun, Red Cloud observed. Why would anyone stay around the cannon long enough to be shot at, when they could ride away?)

On June 6, Red Cloud and the rest of the Oglala delegation were presented to President and Mrs. Grant. Throughout an elegant dinner party shared with officials from many countries in full diplomatic dress, the Indians acquitted themselves well. They drank only a little wine but ate liberal portions of strawberries and ice cream. After the meal, Spotted Tail remarked that he would be glad to turn to farming "if you will always treat me like this."

The next morning, Red Cloud was introduced to his negotiating partner, Secretary of the Interior Jacob Cox. Offering the Lakota leader a chair, Cox told him, "Keep the peace, and then we will do what is right for you." Red Cloud gravely refused the chair and sat cross-legged on the floor. Then he told the secretary,

> Look at me. I was a warrior on this land where the sun rises, now I come from where the sun sets. Whose voice was first sounded on this land—the red people with bows and arrows. The Great Father says he is good and kind to us. I can't see it. . . . I came here to tell the Great Father what I do not like in my country. . . . The white children have surrounded me and have left me nothing but an island. When we first had this land we were strong, now we are melting like snow on the hillside while you are growing like spring grass. . . . I do not want my reservation on the Missouri. This is the fourth time I have said so. . . . Look at me, I am poor and naked. I do not want war with my government. . . . I want you to tell all this to my Great Father.

For the rest of the day, and in the days that followed, Red Cloud repeated his position again and again. Secre-

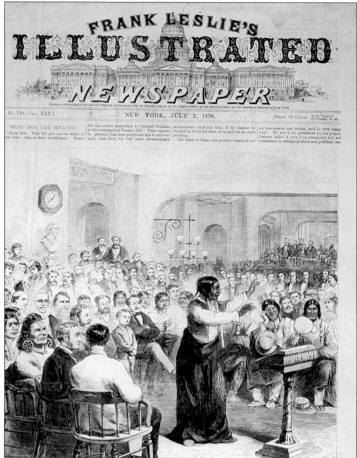

This newspaper illustration shows Red Cloud speaking in the Great Hall of New York City's Cooper Institute. Seated in the foreground are (right to left) an interpreter; Peter Cooper, the institute's founder; and the Oglala leader Red Dog.

tary Cox and his assistants kept telling Red Cloud he had to move to Fort Randall. Red Cloud declared he would not go. They urged him to give up hunting and learn to farm on the reservation. Red Cloud told them he would not go to the reservation until it suited him. They told him the president would send good men to be his agents, traders, teachers, and missionaries. Red Cloud demanded the right to approve these appointments himself.

After days of making no perceivable progress, the government simply submitted. Cox developed a loose interpretation of the Fort Laramie treaty that would allow

Red Cloud and his people to live on their old hunting grounds along the Platte, rather than on the lands near the Missouri that had been set aside for their agency. The Lakotas, Cox announced, could trade at Fort Laramie as long as they were living near it. The Sioux would receive presents now, and later, if they kept the peace, there would be more presents.

Red Cloud proudly turned down the offer of presents but declared he was "pleased" with the results of the negotiations. As the Lakota delegation prepared for their departure, Cox suggested that Red Cloud make a stop in New York City on the way home. Newspapers in New York had already praised Red Cloud for his "frankness and firmness," his "logic . . . pathos . . . and pluck," Cox told him. If he visited the city, he might win even more white support.

Red Cloud reluctantly agreed, and on June 14 he and his delegation arrived in New York. Once again they were shown the sights of a great metropolis. They rode in carriages up Fifth Avenue and through Central Park. In the evening they saw an opulent production at the Grand Opera House.

At noon the next day, Red Cloud addressed the public at the Cooper Institute. Standing at the front of a packed lecture hall, the Lakota leader delivered his speech at a rapid pace, using the elaborate hand gestures common at Lakota councils. The chief's presence held the audience spellbound while his interpreters painstakingly rendered his words into English. Red Cloud told his audience,

> We came to Washington to see our Great Father that peace might be continued. The Great Father that made us both wishes peace to be kept; we want to keep peace. Will you help us? In 1868 men came out and brought papers. We could not read them, and they did not tell us truly what was in them. We thought the treaty was to remove the

forts, and that we should then cease fighting. But they wanted to send us traders on the Missouri. We did not want to go to the Missouri, but wanted traders where we were. All I want is right and just. I have tried to get from the Great Father what is right and just. . . . We do not want riches, but we want to train our children right. Riches would do us no good. . . . The riches that we have in this world, Secretary Cox said truly, we cannot take with us to the next world. Then I wish to know why Commissioners are sent out to us who do nothing but rob us and get the riches of this world away from us? . . . I have sent a great many words to the Great Father, but they never reached him. They were drowned on the way, and I was afraid the words I spoke lately to the Great Father would not reach you. So I came to speak to you myself; and now I am going away to my home.

Indians and officials gather outside government offices at the Red Cloud agency in 1876. Red Cloud agreed to move his encampment to this site after a long argument with government authorities.

Red Cloud returned to Fort Laramie at the end of June. That summer, he showed his faith in the government's promises by urging his allies to abide by the terms of the 1868 treaty. It was the most peaceful summer the Platte River valley had seen in many years.

Yet no sooner had the Oglala leader left the capital than U.S. officials began to change their plans. Over the next three years, government agents continued to press Red Cloud to move his people away from Fort Laramie.

Finally, in 1873, he agreed to resettle at an agency about 100 miles northeast of the fort, on the White River. Gradually he persuaded his people to follow him there.

After more than five years of resisting the U.S. government, the Oglala leader settled in peacefully at his new home, Red Cloud Agency. His decision to move at this time may well have been a practical one. For between government councils, Red Cloud had traveled widely through Lakota country, and he had seen that his land had been transformed. The buffalo—the foundation of Lakota life—were disappearing so quickly that if Red Cloud's people continued to try to live by hunting, they would starve.

The buffalo were not simply dying out; they were being systematically slaughtered. Bounties were being offered for buffalo hides. Sportsmen could ride a train to the edge of the giant buffalo herd and shoot the animals down from the windows, leaving their carcasses to rot in the sun. By the mid-1870s, the great herds that had once

Buffalo carcasses litter the plains in 1872. After an eastern tannery decided to use buffalo as a source of commercial leather, hunters began slaughtering the animals at the rate of 3 million a year, destroying the foundation of Lakota culture.

darkened wide stretches of Lakota territory had virtually vanished.

Red Cloud may have believed that his people could never survive unless they accepted the assistance the government was offering them at the White River agency. Once established there, he seemed prepared to adapt to the life the agents had laid out for him. For the most part, he stayed away from the Powder River country—the very land he had fought so hard to defend—and continued to negotiate peacefully for the advancement of his Oglala followers.

His peace would not last long, however, for the conflict between the Sioux nation and the U.S. government was not yet over. Red Cloud may have put away his arms, but Crazy Horse, Sitting Bull, and thousands of other Lakotas—many of whom had never signed the Treaty of 1868—were still avoiding the agencies and hunting in the lands northwest of the Black Hills, where the great buffalo herds had not yet been depleted. These men showed no interest in the goods and services U.S. officials were offering at Red Cloud Agency, and if the government ever threatened to take away their hunting grounds, they were ready to fight to protect them.

Soon enough, the time for fighting came. In 1874, about the time Red Cloud's people were making their reluctant move to the White River, the U.S. Army sent an expedition to the Black Hills to investigate miners' claims that large reserves of gold were to be found there. The Black Hills—known to the Lakotas as Pa Sapa—were an essential part of the "unceded territory" the Indians had been promised in the Treaty of 1868. Yet when the expedition returned from the region with reports of "gold among the grassroots," Washington officials immediately set out to take the land away.

In 1875, the president sent a party of officials to Red Cloud Agency to negotiate for the purchase of the Black Hills. Senator William Allison, the leader of this commission, planned to offer the Lakotas as much as $6 million for the region. Much to the surprise of the Allison commission, both Red Cloud and Spotted Tail were prepared to sell. What they asked for in return, however, was a sum much larger then the commissioners had envisioned. Red Cloud told the commission:

> For seven generations to come I want our Great Father to give us Texan steers for our meat. I want the Government to issue for me hereafter, flour and coffee, and sugar and tea, and bacon, the very best kind, and cracked corn and beans, and rice and dried apples, and saleratus and tobacco, and soap and salt, and pepper, for the old people. I want a wagon, a light wagon with a span of horses, and six yoke of working cattle for my people. I want a sow and a boar, and a cow and bull, and a sheep and a ram, and a hen and a cock, for each family. I am an Indian, but you try to make a white man out of me. I want some white men's houses at this agency to be built for the Indians. I have been into white people's houses, and I have seen nice black bedsteads and chairs, and I want that kind of furniture given to my people. . . . I want the Great Father to furnish me a sawmill which I may call my own. I want a mower and a scythe for my people. Maybe you white people think that I ask too much from the Government, but I think those hills extend clear to the sky—maybe they go above the sky, and that is the reason I ask for so much.

This price, according to Allison, was "far beyond any sum that could possibly be considered by the Government," and the commission retreated in defeat.

Meanwhile, Red Cloud's willingness to negotiate with the Allison commission angered many of the younger Lakotas at the agency, and later that year hundreds of them drifted north to join Sitting Bull, Crazy Horse, and their followers. Disturbed by reports that large bands of

hostile Sioux were gathering west of the Black Hills, and frustrated by their failure to obtain the lands they wanted through diplomacy, U.S. officials finally launched a full-scale assault on the Lakotas.

On December 3, 1875, Commissioner of Indian Affairs Edward P. Smith announced that any Indian who did not report to the agencies by January 31 would be hunted down by the U.S. Army. In February 1876, when most of the hunting bands had failed to come in, the last of the U.S.–Indian wars broke out in the lands between the Black Hills and the Bighorn Mountains. It culminated in one of the most infamous defeats in the history of the U.S. Army: the fall of General George Armstrong Custer and his 220-man command at the Battle of the Little Bighorn. Red Cloud, who had sworn at the council of

In 1876, this commission, chaired by I. W. Manypenny (center), forced Red Cloud, Spotted Tail, and other agency Sioux to sell the Black Hills by threatening to withdraw their rations. Most of the Indians who signed the document authorizing the sale later told officials they had not understood it.

1868 never again to wage war, remained at Red Cloud Agency for the duration of the fighting. According to some accounts, however, his son Jack joined Crazy Horse's forces and fought in the battle known to many as Custer's Last Stand.

Whatever vicarious triumph Red Cloud may have felt over the Little Bighorn victory was short-lived. Within days of the battle, the army had declared martial law throughout the Sioux agencies. Announcing that the Indians had broken the Treaty of 1868 by attacking the U.S. Army, a government commission coerced Red Cloud, Spotted Tail, and several other agency Sioux into signing a new document giving up the tribe's rights to the Black Hills and the Powder River country. Meanwhile, Red Cloud's people were ordered to move to a new agency located on the Missouri River.

In August, all the men at Red Cloud Agency were arrested, deprived of their guns and their horses, and marched to the nearest army post, Fort Robinson. There the commanding officer, General George Crook, who was convinced that Red Cloud had been supplying the northern bands with ammunition and encouraging his people to join their cause, stripped Red Cloud of his chieftaincy and made Spotted Tail chief of all the Sioux.

This demotion could have no real effect, for in the Lakota tradition, a chief's power lay in the trust of his people. Red Cloud knew that his followers, the Oglalas, would never defect to the Brulé leader Spotted Tail unless they had lost confidence in his own abilities. Indeed, only a few weeks after his removal, Red Cloud resumed his official position as head of the Oglala agency. Crook's impulsive action had only served to deepen the gulf of mistrust that lay between Red Cloud and the U.S. government.

7

"LIKE SNOW ON THE HILLSIDE"

Winter was setting in when Red Cloud and his followers—some 8,000 Indians in all—began their move to the new Missouri River agency. Many of the Indians were ill, and early snows soon added to their suffering. When the group reached a spot along the White River about 100 miles west of the Missouri, some 2,000 Indians broke free from their army escorts and headed north, where Sitting Bull—who had not yet turned himself in—was said to have his encampment. Red Cloud, meanwhile, announced that he would go no farther.

For the next two years, while U.S. officials decided whether to force them to proceed, Red Cloud and his people remained at this encampment, midway between the old agency and the new. Finally, after the Lakota leader petitioned the government several times for an agency farther west, his people were allowed to settle on the White Clay River. This spot, which the whites named Pine Ridge Agency, was to remain Red Cloud's home for the rest of his life.

In 1879, Dr. Valentine T. McGillycuddy took charge of the newly established Pine Ridge Agency, and he quickly set out to transform the life of the Oglala Sioux. A firm believer in the value of "civilization," McGilly-

Red Cloud holds a feathered pipe and a beaded bag in this portrait from the mid-1880s.

cuddy spent much of his first year trying to persuade the Indians to stop living near the agency and move into the open country, where they could support themselves by farming. Eventually there would be no more government provisions, he told them, and they would have to fend for themselves. The sooner they learned how to farm, the better.

Red Cloud, who may well have seen the agent as a threat to his own authority, objected vehemently. "The Great Spirit did not make us to work," he told McGilly-cuddy. "He made us to hunt and fish. He gave us the great prairies and hills and covered them with buffalo, deer, and antelope. He filled the rivers and streams with fish. The white man can work if he wants to, but the

An 1891 photograph shows a Lakota encampment at Pine Ridge Agency, established for Red Cloud and his followers in 1879. The agency's name was adopted in order to avoid association with the troublesome Red Cloud Agency, though the area had no ridge and very few pines.

Great Spirit did not make us to work. The white man owes us a living for the lands he has taken from us."

Soon after this encounter, Red Cloud and 21 other Oglala chiefs signed a letter to the president asking for the removal of McGillycuddy, but nothing came of their request. More disputes followed, and McGillycuddy soon came to see Red Cloud—quite correctly—as an impediment to his carefully laid out plans. He told his superiors that the leader was resisting "progress," and that the Oglalas gave him much more respect than he deserved. To McGillycuddy, Red Cloud and Spotted Tail together formed "as egregious a pair of old frauds . . . as it has ever been my fortune or misfortune to encounter."

By September 1880, McGillycuddy was convinced that Red Cloud was losing favor with the younger men at Pine Ridge Agency, and he called a council and invited the Lakotas to vote Red Cloud out of office. McGillycuddy thought that the ambitious young Sioux would be eager to supplant the aging chief. But put to a vote, more than 95 percent of the men at the council wanted Red Cloud to remain as their leader. "Red Cloud was chosen almost without opposition," said American Horse, a younger council member, afterward. "He has been our head chief, he is now and always will be, because the Nation love, respect and believe in him."

When his attempt at a democratic solution failed, McGillycuddy abandoned democracy and deposed Red Cloud on his own authority. Although the agent took to referring to Red Cloud as the "former chief" in official correspondence, the Indians ignored his gesture, just as they had when the leader was demoted by Crook four years earlier.

McGillycuddy encountered further resistance from Red Cloud in February 1881, when he tried to conduct a census—an exact count of the number of people living

on the reservation. Although the agent perceived the chief's defiance as stubborn and arbitrary, in this case Red Cloud may have had practical reasons for his opposition. The amount of goods the government distributed at each agency depended on how many people lived there, and there were almost certainly fewer Oglalas at Pine Ridge than the 15,000 officially listed. As far as Red Cloud was concerned, the Indians' provisions were already inadequate. They could not afford a reduction. Yet when he tried to prevent the count, McGillycuddy withheld the food that was to be delivered to his family and the 27 other Oglala families who lived near him, and after a week the chief relented. Fortunately for the Sioux, this census was still so inaccurate that their rations were not affected.

Meanwhile, Red Cloud repeated his efforts to bring about the agent's removal. In August 1882, the chief and several of his people signed a letter to the secretary of the interior stating, "if the incumbent as U.S. Agent is not removed from this agency within 60 days . . . we will take upon ourselves the responsibility of politely escorting him out of our country."

Finally, after almost three years of charges and countercharges, the Bureau of Indian Affairs sent an inspector to investigate the situation. He sided with Red Cloud, for, as he put it, "It could hardly be expected that the old chief would work in harmony with a man who lost no opportunity to humiliate and to heap indignity upon him, who called him liar, fool, squaw, refused to shake hands with, deposed him, ordered the agency employees not to entertain him in their houses." According to historian James Olsen, the inspector found that McGillycuddy was "living high at the expense of the Indians, had taken credit on vouchers that were not paid, . . . had unlawfully deprived Red Cloud of rations while giving the Indian

Dr. Valentine T. McGillycuddy holds a sextant in this photograph taken during a surveying expedition in the early 1870s. McGillycuddy later became an agent at Pine Ridge, where he clashed with Red Cloud and other Lakota leaders.

police and other favorites more than they could use . . . [and] had permitted agency employees to convert government supplies to their own use." But when the commissioner for Indian affairs followed up these charges, he found McGillycuddy guilty only of "technical irregularities" and allowed him to keep his office.

Even as the conflict between Red Cloud and McGillycuddy was taking its sordid course, government officials were preparing to wrest yet another tract of land from

Red Cloud leads an Oglala delegation to Washington to discuss conflicts with McGillycuddy in 1880. Seated in front of government official John Bridgeman are (left to right) Red Dog, Little Wound, Red Cloud, American Horse, and Red Shirt.

the Sioux. This time, the committee charged with appropriating the land ignored the rule that called for three-fourths of all males to agree to a treaty amendment. They simply went to the agencies and offered the chiefs their proposal. The Lakotas were to cede about 11 million acres: all their land between the White and Cheyenne rivers, as well as all their territory north of the Cheyenne and west of the 102nd meridian. Their remaining land would be broken up into five separate reservations, each dedicated to a single subtribe of the Sioux. Each Indian family was to be granted 320 acres of land for farming. The government would also supply the Indians with about 26,000 head of cattle.

In explaining the treaty to the Sioux, McGillycuddy apparently neglected to explain that a large tract of land would have to be given away in return for the cattle. According to some reports, he told the Oglalas that they would lose their land if they did *not* sign the new agreement.

Red Cloud, who had already seen the Fort Laramie treaty renegotiated three times, argued bitterly against the treaty. But the young men prevailed in council, and many of them signed it. While the commission moved on to the surrounding agencies to seek further signatures, however, the U.S. Senate learned that the negotiations were not being carried out according to the provisions of the Treaty of 1868. More signatures would be needed at Pine Ridge before the deal could go through.

Red Cloud was happy to hear this news, for he knew that the commission could never obtain an accurate count of the adult male population at Pine Ridge. The Oglala chief tried to press his advantage with the help of Dr. T. A. Bland, a noted supporter of Indian rights. When a Democratic administration took over in Washington, the pair put forth enough pressure to cause another investigation into McGillycuddy's alleged offenses. Even this committee could not pin any specific charges on the agent, but, perhaps buckling under their pressure, he resigned a few weeks later.

Red Cloud had outlasted his opponent, and now he was ready for peace. "We must become as one nation," he told a white audience on July 4, 1886. "With one heart and one mind. We will build our two houses into one." Shortly after McGillycuddy's departure, Red Cloud permitted the army to take a more accurate census. The official reservation count was placed at 4,873, a cut of almost 3,000 from the earlier figure used by McGillycuddy. It meant a 40 percent reduction in the Indians' rations, and the new Pine Ridge agent, H. D. Gallagher, quietly made the cuts with little opposition from the Sioux.

Two years later, the U.S. government resumed its quest for the Indians' land. In September 1888, Congress passed a bill authorizing the purchase of the territory outlined by the commission of 1882, this time at a price of 50 cents an acre. Virtually all of the Lakotas opposed this proposition. To gain their favor, the government once again invited a Sioux delegation to Washington to meet with the president. This time U.S. officials ignored both Red Cloud and another outspoken Oglala, Young Man Afraid of His Horse, and concentrated instead on securing the signatures of the less recalcitrant leaders.

The Lakota delegation was able to negotiate a slightly higher price for the land, but not to put a stop to the purchase. Sensing that his hard-won territory was once more slipping away, Red Cloud traveled to Washington at his own expense in order to discuss the matter with the secretary of the Interior, but his efforts were in vain.

When the time came to secure the approval of the Indians at Pine Ridge, however, the government found

*Emblems of two cultures
adorn Red Cloud's bedroom
at Pine Ridge Agency.*

them resistant. A council was held at the agency on June 17, and, along with 600 other Lakotas, Red Cloud came with a map of the reservation. He told the commission:

> This is the map that the Great Father laid out for me for a reservation, and I am living on it. . . . We made up another treaty and gave up the right to hunt down at the Republican River, and we got $25,000, and during that time the Government promised to try and get $25,000 more for us. The next treaty we made was with Colonel Manypenny at my agency and Spotted Tail Agency. At that time we agreed to let him have the Black Hills, just the top of them. In that treaty, I asked for pay for seven generations. . . . Now you come here and ask for more land. You want to buy more land, and I looked around to see if I could see any boxes of money that you brought here to buy more land, and I could not see any, and now I think this is the talk of sugar again just as this paper was.

Although he attended the rest of the meetings, Red Cloud did not speak again. At the end of June, some 700 of the Pine Ridge Indians had signed away the land. Although this figure fell far short of what the Treaty of 1868 required, the Sioux Act of 1889 was soon passed.

By the time the treaty went to Washington, the Lakotas at Pine Ridge Agency were suffering from

Pine Ridge Agency women wait for rations on a cold winter day in 1891. The Lakotas endured two drastic cutbacks in government food distribution between 1886 and 1890.

hunger and confusion. They returned from the summer councils to find that drought and disease had killed off much of their livestock and what planting they had begun. Soon after this their rations were again cut by almost half. The Lakotas looked to Red Cloud for guidance, but he had little to offer. Destitute, the Indians turned to a new religion for relief.

8

THE END OF THE ROAD

Red Cloud was nearing the age of 70 when word reached him that the Messiah had come. Far to the west, among the Paiute Indians of the southern plains, a holy man named Wovoka was spreading hope to Indians across the country.

Wovoka was telling his people that in a few years all the Indians who had perished in war or famine would return, and the world would once more be rich and green. The Indians needed only to perform a special dance, known as the Ghost Dance, in order to evoke these changes. Dancers were to wear a feather that would mark them as believers and wear a white shirt that would protect them from all harm. During the dance, men and women were to stand in a circle, facing inward and holding hands. They were to sing with no accompaniment, not even drums. The dance was supposed to go on until, one by one, the dancers dropped in their tracks, fainting from exhaustion.

If the Indians followed these instructions, Wovoka promised, great things would happen. A great flood would come to wash away the evils of the world. The earth would roll up, taking with it the white man's civilization: its industry, its farming, its buildings. Underneath would be a new green world for the Indians alone. The Indians'

Lines of sorrow, strength, and experience mark Red Cloud's face in this photograph from the early 1900s.

dead would return to life, and the white men would go back to their land beyond the oceans. All this was to happen by the end of 1890.

When Wovoka's message of renewal reached Pine Ridge Agency in 1889, it struck a chord in the hearts of the Lakotas. Hundreds of Red Cloud's people abandoned their farms and the white man's schools to practice the new religion. Red Cloud himself did not participate in the Ghost Dance, but he may well have supported its spirit, and his son Jack became one of the movement's leaders.

Although Wovoka preached nonviolence—telling, in fact, of days when the Indians would give up all war—the Ghost Dance ritual made many whites uneasy. Some considered it blasphemy. Others could see that it inspired in the Indians feelings of independence, and they worried that this new-found autonomy would lead the tribe back to the fighting ways of the past.

An American flag flies above Red Cloud's home at Pine Ridge Agency. In 1890, when the Ghost Dance movement was at its peak, many dancers camped near here, hoping Red Cloud's influence with the government would protect them from persecution.

For his part, the Pine Ridge agent, H. D. Gallagher, seemed undisturbed by the movement. In June 1890, he wrote his superiors that the Indians were gathering for the Ghost Dance without his consent, but he was certain the activity would soon die out.

But in October, Gallagher was replaced by D. F. Royer, described by one of his colleagues as "a gentleman totally ignorant of the Indians and their peculiarities." The Ghost Dance completely unnerved the new agent. He met with Red Cloud and the other chiefs of the reservation in early November to try and persuade them to give up the Ghost Dance. Little Wound, Red Cloud, and the others simply laughed at him.

By mid-November, Royer was frantically wiring to Washington for troops to protect the area and arrest the leaders of the movement. "Indians are dancing in the snow and are wild and crazy," he telegraphed. "Why delay by further investigation, we need protection and we need it now. The leaders should be arrested and confined at some military post until the matter is quieted and this should be done at once." Toward the end of the month, 8,000 soldiers, under the command of Generals Nelson Miles and John Brooke, arrived in South Dakota and set up camp near the agencies.

James McLaughlin, the agent at Standing Rock Agency, reported that Sitting Bull was the chief cause of the unrest in that part of the country, and on December 15, a party of Indian policemen went out to arrest the Hunkpapa chief. When his followers tried to come to his aid, a skirmish ensued, and Sitting Bull and 14 others were killed.

Sitting Bull's death caused anger and deep distress among the Lakotas. Yet the Ghost Dancers still believed that if they could keep up the dance for a few more weeks, the world change would be upon them. Red Cloud, meanwhile, grew disenchanted with the movement and persuaded his son Jack to give it up. When yet another purported holy man—a settler dressed in Indian clothes and claiming to be the Messiah—arrived at the reservation, Red Cloud spat in his face. "Go home," he said. "You are no Son of God."

By mid-December, some 2,000 members of the movement had fled the army and set up camp to the north in the Dakota Bad Lands. Tensions mounted as the dance continued. According to the commander of the Nebraska National Guard, "Great lights and signal fires shone from the bluffs and hill tops a few miles distant from Pine Ridge, and the Bad Lands were ablaze with lights that could be seen for miles."

On December 28, a party of troops under Colonel James Forsyth surrounded some 300 men, women, and children from the Cheyenne River Agency at their camp near Porcupine Creek. Big Foot, the leader of the band, immediately surrendered, and the Indians were marched toward Pine Ridge. They halted for the night next to Wounded Knee Creek, and the next morning Forsyth ordered the Indians to give up their arms. Most of the Lakotas reluctantly complied, but somehow, as the troops searched their tipis for axes and knives, a soldier heard what he thought was a gunshot, and the cavalry opened fire on the unarmed Sioux. Big Foot and several others were killed in the first volley. Others tried to flee, only to be shot to pieces by the army's Hotchkiss guns. Only about 50 Indians survived.

News of the massacre at Wounded Knee spread terror and hostility among the Lakotas. Some of the Ghost Dancers, on their way to Pine Ridge, retreated when they heard of the tragedy. Others had already returned to the agency, and when they heard of the assault, they threatened to take action. A few days after the Wounded Knee incident, Two Strike, a Brulé chief who was camped near Red Cloud's house, opened fire on the agency buildings, wounding two soldiers. Then the Brulés fled, taking Red Cloud and his family with them.

By January 1 some 3,000 Indians had fled Pine Ridge and gathered at White Clay Creek, a few miles to the north of the agency. General Miles arrived at the agency soon afterward. Hoping to bring the Lakotas in without a battle, he sent placating messages to the Indians' camp, telling them that they would not be harmed. "I know all the wrongs that have been done to the Indians and the wrongs the Indians have done. If they do whatever I tell them it will be the best for all the Indians." Not surprisingly, after the events at Wounded Knee, most of the Lakotas were in no mood to listen.

The Indians held a series of councils, during which Red Cloud argued that they should yield to Miles, but "that crazy boy," as he later called Two Strike, refused.

A burial party gathers the dead after the massacre at Wounded Knee. With them was Dr. Charles Eastman, the Pine Ridge doctor, who was himself a Santee Sioux. "Among the fragments of burned tents and other belongings we saw the frozen bodies lying close together or piled one upon another," he later wrote. "I counted eighty bodies of men . . . who were almost as helpless as the women and the babes when the deadly fire began."

After the Wounded Knee massacre, Two Strike, Crow Dog, and High Hawk (pictured, left to right) inspired more than 3,000 Lakotas to flee Pine Ridge Agency. On January 16, 1891, they followed Red Cloud's example and surrendered to General Nelson Miles.

He vowed that they would all die together, and that he would kill the first man to try and escape. Fearing for his life, the old chief escaped from the camp, seeking refuge with Miles and his men. "I tried my best for them to let me go back," he later explained, "but they would not let me go, and said if I went, they would kill me. I and my family . . . made our escape very late in the night while they were all asleep."

The events at White Clay Creek ended not with a battle, but with the quiet return to order that should have happened at Wounded Knee. Miles showed his good faith by demanding the removal of Royer, the agent who had started the panic, and replacing him with another man the Lakotas knew and trusted. After several weeks of negotiations, the Indians surrendered, and for the most part returned to their former lives. A few of their leaders were arrested, including Sitting Bull's old friend Kicking Bear, but they were soon released. A delegation was sent to Washington to discuss the events—Red Cloud was not among them—and more papers were issued. Under the slow, grinding wheels of government bureaucracy, the last great Sioux uprising of the 19th century came to a close.

The massacre at Wounded Knee and its aftermath was the last major conflict in Red Cloud's life. Age and failing eyesight accomplished what hostile tribes, the U.S. Army, and government agents could not. By the early 1890s, Red Cloud was losing power among his people.

To be sure, he continued to make his voice heard in council, and even in Washington, for the next 20 years. He traveled east on one or two more occasions and sometimes met with government representatives closer to home. He still agitated for what he considered his people's rights, from changes in the reservation's judicial system to the prompt payment of land fees and annuities. He was prepared at a moment's notice to recount a list of his people's grievances. Red Cloud had a good memory, and the recitation could take a long time.

But most of his time was spent near the healing waters of the Shoshone reservation, or with Captain James Cook, a frontiersman who had befriended him after his move to the reservation. Once when he was on his way to the Shoshones, Red Cloud was arrested for poaching on the land upon which he had hunted freely for most of his life. To Red Cloud's lasting embarrassment, Jack had to sell a team of horses to pay for his release from prison.

Slowly, Red Cloud entered a quiet, sometimes frustrated retirement. "We have trouble," he told a friend one day. "Our girls are getting bad. Coughing sickness every winter carries away our best people. My heart is heavy. I am old. I cannot do much more."

Red Cloud's transformation from man to legend was complete before his death. To the Lakotas, he remained a living link to the days when the tribe hunted and waged war on the open plains. His people respected him, but they believed that the wisdom he had to offer had little to do with the road ahead of them.

*Approaching the age of 90,
Red Cloud joins his grand-
daughter and his son Jack
outside his Pine Ridge home.*

Around 1909, a group of historians invited Red Cloud
back to his old lands near the Powder River. They were
erecting a small memorial at the site of the Fetterman
massacre, and they wanted the men who had witnessed
the battle to be there. Colonel Carrington came, but Red
Cloud could not. His failing health prevented him from
reversing the path he had traveled over the past 40 years,
though he sent a message of regret. It would have been
an honor, he said, to shake the hand of his great enemy.

Red Cloud died at his Pine Ridge home on December
10, 1909. Although still honored among his people, at the

time of his death he had been all but forgotten by the U.S. government. The wars of the plains were long over, and there was little time to remember a long-defeated foe.

In the days of Red Cloud's youth, the death of a chief of the Great Plains was marked by special rituals. Among some tribes, relatives would cut their hair, paint themselves in mourning colors, and perhaps even wound themselves in their grief. Red Cloud, however, had converted to Catholicism in his later years, and he was buried with the rites of the Catholic Church at the Holy Rosary Mission at Pine Ridge. There his grave remains to this day.

At the end of his life, Red Cloud may have believed that his long fight to preserve Lakota tradition had ended in failure. Indeed, a year after his burial, his friend James Cook wrote,

> The younger people among the Sioux have taken to the white man's road, to the extent that it is now as unpopular for one of them to appear wild and untameable, as it was a very short time ago for any young man or woman to assume the white people's style of dress or hair cut. Some have advanced so far along the lines of civilization that they are almost ashamed of their old fathers and mothers, and their primitive habits and customs.

Yet 50 years later, the Sioux Nation began a cultural revival that has carried through to the present. The Lakotas have recovered many of their old traditions, and they continue to assert their independence, fighting to regain the rights the U.S. government has long denied them. As they move toward the future, today's Lakota leaders also look back to the men and women of their tribe who struggled for freedom before them. Sometime in the early 1970s, a young Lakota visiting Red Cloud's grave left behind a circled cross, the symbol of his people.

CHRONOLOGY

ca. 1822   Born near the forks of the Platte River in western Nebraska

1841   Kills Bull Bear, chief of the Koya Oglalas

ca. 1842   Leads his first war party; marries Pretty Owl

1851   Plains tribes meet government agents at the first Fort Laramie treaty council; Indians grant settlers right of way through their territory in exchange for a government annuity

1854   U.S. troops kill Conquering Bear, chief of the Sioux, at Fort Laramie; Brulé and Oglala warriors kill John L. Grattan and 29 of his men in the so-called Grattan massacre

1855   General William S. Harney kills 86 Indians camped with Brulé chief Little Thunder on the Bluewater River

1864   Colorado volunteers under Colonel John H. Chivington kill 130 Cheyennes at Sand Creek, Colorado

1866   Red Cloud's warriors lay siege to Fort Phil Kearny; in December, they wipe out Captain William Fetterman and his 80-man command

1867   U.S. troops repulse Red Cloud's forces in the Wagon Box Fight near Fort Phil Kearny

1868   Red Cloud signs treaty ending warfare; U.S. government agrees to withdraw troops from Lakota lands near the Powder River

1870   Red Cloud travels to Washington to negotiate for trading rights at Fort Laramie

1873   Settles at Red Cloud Agency on the White River

1876   Lakota, Cheyenne, and Arapaho forces destroy General George Armstrong Custer and his men at the Battle of the Little Bighorn; accused of supporting the campaign, Red Cloud and his followers are arrested

1878   Red Cloud's people move to Pine Ridge Agency on the White Clay River

1889   U.S. officials persuade the Sioux to relinquish 11 million acres of land to non-Indian settlers

1890   U.S. troops under Colonel James Forsyth kill more than 150 Lakotas at Wounded Knee Creek

1909   Red Cloud dies at Pine Ridge Agency

FURTHER READING

Brandon, William. *Indians.* Boston: Houghton Mifflin, 1961.

Brininstool, E. A., *Fighting Indian Warriors: True Tales of the Wild Frontiers.* New York: Crown, 1953.

Brown, Dee. *Bury My Heart at Wounded Knee.* New York: Holt, Rinehart & Winston, 1970.

Erdoes, Richard. *The Sun Dance People: The Plains Indians, Their Past & Present.* New York: Knopf, 1972.

Garst, Shannon. *Red Cloud.* Chicago: Follett, 1965.

Gidley, M. *With One Sky Above Us: Life on an Indian Reservation at the Turn of the Century.* New York: G. P. Putnam's Sons, 1979.

Goble, Paul, and Dorothy Goble. *Brave Eagle's Account of the Fetterman Fight.* New York: Random House, 1972.

Guttmacher, Peter. *Crazy Horse: Sioux War Chief.* New York: Chelsea House, 1994.

Longstreet, Stephen. *War Cries on Horseback: The Story of the Indian Wars on the Great Plains.* Garden City, NY: Doubleday, 1970.

McGaa, Ed. *Red Cloud: The Story of an American Indian.* Minneapolis: Dillon Press, 1971.

Olson, James C. *Red Cloud and the Sioux Problem.* Lincoln: University of Nebraska Press, 1965.

Parker, Watson. *Gold in the Black Hills.* Norman: University of Oklahoma Press, 1966.

INDEX

Mankata, Minnesota, 53
Miles, Nelson, 99, 101, 102
Minneconjou Teton Sioux
    Indians, 15, 16, 22, 47, 48,
    63
Minnesota, 21, 22, 52, 53
Missouri River, 21, 22, 23, 50,
    73, 74, 75, 77, 78, 83, 85
Montana, 12, 52, 58

Nebraska, 12, 21, 22
No-Bow Teton Sioux Indians,
    22, 51, 63, 70
North Dakota, 22, 53

Oglala Teton Sioux Indians,
    21, 35, 38, 40, 41, 45, 48,
    49, 50, 51, 52, 54, 56, 63,
    70, 73, 74, 75, 78, 80, 83,
    85, 87, 89, 92
Ojibwa Indians, 22
Oregon Trail, 40, 41, 42, 47,
    48, 57

Paiute Indians, 97
Pawnee Indians, 25, 31, 38, 50
Pine Leaf, 39
Pine Ridge Agency, 85, 87,
    89, 91, 92, 94, 98, 99, 100,
    101, 104
Platte Bridge Station, 57
Platte River, 35, 37, 38, 48,
    49, 54, 77
Platte River Valley, 39, 47,
    50, 68, 78
Powder River, 56, 57, 58, 59,
    64, 65, 71, 73, 80, 83, 104
Pretty Owl (wife), 38, 39

Red Cloud (father), 21, 31
Red Cloud
    birth, 21
    Catholicism, converts to, 105
    childhood, 23–33

death, 104–5
and Ghost Dance, 95,
    97–103
and Grand Teton Council,
    50–52
as healer, 41
Valentine McGillycuddy,
    feud with, 85–92
marraiges, 38–39
Red Cloud's war, 11–19,
    63–71, 104
on reservation, 79–105
trips to East coast, 74–78,
    92, 103
vision quest, 29–30
warfare with Indian tribes,
    31, 36–38
warfare with whites, 11–19,
    56–71
Red Cloud Agency, 79, 80, 81,
    83
Roman Nose (Cheyenne
    chief), 57
Royer, D. F., 99, 102

Sand Creek massacre, 54–56
Santee Sioux Indians, 52, 53
Santee uprising, 52–53, 54
Sherman, William T., 19, 69
Shoshone Indians, 42, 44, 52
Shoshone Reservation, 103
Sioux Act of 1889, 94
Sioux Indians, 25, 30, 31, 35,
    36, 38, 39, 40, 77
    and Black Hills, 80–83
    and buffalo, 26–28, 79–80
    epidemics, 41
    and Ghost Dance, 95, 97–102
    history, 21–23
    and horses, 28–29
    reservation life, 85–105
    treaties, 42–45, 50, 63, 69–
        71, 73, 76, 78, 80, 83,
        91, 93, 94

warfare with whites, 11–19,
    47–69, 82, 100,
Sitting Bull (Hunkpapa Sioux
    chief), 51, 80, 81, 85, 99,
    102
Smoke (Bad Face Oglala
    Teton Sioux chief), 48, 59,
    74, 75, 81, 83, 87
Spotted Tail Agency, 93
Standing Rock Agency, 99
Stony Lake, Battle of, 53

Teton Sioux Indians, 22, 23,
    28, 33, 44, 50
Treaty of 1868, 71, 73, 78, 80,
    83, 91, 94
Two-Kettle Teton Sioux
    Indians, 22, 51
Two Moon (Cheyenne chief),
    66
Two Strike (Brulé sioux
    chief), 101

U.S. government, 41, 42, 44,
    49, 56, 58, 63, 71, 75, 80,
    81, 90, 91, 103, 105
Ute Indians, 32

Wagon Box Fight, 68
Walks As She Thinks
    (mother), 21, 23, 31
Washington D.C., 59, 74, 77,
    91, 92, 94, 99, 102, 103
White River, 41, 79, 80, 85,
    91
White River Agency, 80
Wounded Knee, massacre at,
    100, 101, 103
Wovoka, 97, 98
Wyoming, 22, 35

Young Man Afraid of His
    Horse, 57, 92

PICTURE CREDITS

JERRY LAZAR has been a writer and editor for a dozen years, covering such diverse topics as computers, music, and the law. He has also worked as a musician, playwright, and actor. Lazar lives in New Jersey with his wife and two children.

W. DAVID BAIRD is the Howard A. White Professor of History at Pepperdine University in Malibu, California. He holds a Ph.D. from the University of Oklahoma and was formerly on the faculty of history at the University of Arkansas, Fayetteville, and Oklahoma State University. He has served as president of both the Western History Association, a professional organization, and Phi Alpha Theta, the international honor society for students of history. Dr. Baird is also the author of *The Quapaw Indians: A History of the Downstream People* and *Peter Pitchlynn: Chief of the Choctaws* and the editor of *A Creek Warrior of the Confederacy: The Autobiography of Chief G. W. Grayson.*